DUB POETS IN THEIR OWN WORDS

ERIC DOUMERC

A journey allowing dub poets to explore the debates and controversies plaguing their art form over the years. The interviews here were conducted in Britain, Canada, Jamaica and the USA with Yasus Afari, Klyde Broox, Dreadlockalien, Mbala, Mutabaruka, Cherry Natural, Kokumo Noxid, Oku Onuora, Moqapi Selassie and Malachi D Smith by Eric Doumerc of the University of Toulouse.

Dub Poets In Their Own Words

Some interviews originally appeared in various academic journals. And are reproduced courtesy of *The Journal of Commonwealth Literature*, *Jamaica Journal*, *Macomere* and *The Journal of West Indian Literature:*
"From Page-Poet to Recording Artist: Mutabaruka interviewed by Eric Doumerc", *The Journal of Commonwealth Literature*, Vol. 44, N° 3, 2009.
"An Interview with Mbala: A Dub Poet's Innerverse", *Jamaica Journal,* Vol.33, N° 1 and 2, 2010.
"In Conversation with Cherry Natural: From the Page to the Stage ". *Macomere*, Vols 1 and 2, 2011- 2012.
"An Interview with Malachi Smith". *The Journal of West Indian Literature*, Vol.22 N0. 1, November 2013

Front cover illustration by kind permission of Mbala

APS Publications
www.andrewsparke.com

CONTENTS

DUB POETRY: AN OVERVIEW

The words "dub poetry" refer to a particular type of "performance poetry", a brand of oral poetry performed to the accompaniment of reggae music. It seems that the phrase "dub poetry" was used for the first time in 1975 by the poet Linton Kwesi Johnson in an article about Jamaican deejays which was published in *Race and Class*: "The "dub-lyricist" is the dj turned poet. He intones his lyrics rather than sings them. Dub-lyricism is a new form of (oral) music-poetry wherein the lyricist overdubs rhythmic phrases on to the rhythm background of a popular song. Dub-lyricists include poets like Big Youth, I Roy, U Roy, Dillinger, Shorty the President, Prince Jazzbo and others" (Johnson 1976*)*.

Around the same time, in Jamaica a young poet named Orlando Wong (who later took on the nom de plume Oku Onuora) was developing a type of oral poetry which had been influenced by the African-American poets Langston Hughes, Gil Scott-Heron and The Last Poets, and by reggae lyricism (Morris 1997).

From 1979 on, the phrase "dub poetry" was increasingly used to refer to an artistic and cultural movement which had been developing at the Jamaica School of Drama for a few years and which was associated with poets like Oku Onuora himself, Noel Walcott and Michael Smith, among others.

Oku Onuora defined the term in an interview conducted with the poet and critic Mervyn Morris in 1979 and stated that a dub poem was "a poem that has a built-in reggae rhythm - hence when the poem is read without any reggae rhythm (so to speak) backing, one can distinctly hear the reggae rhythm coming out of the poem" (Brown 51-54). So a dub poem is a poem that relies on a reggae rhythm that can be heard even when there is no musical accompaniment. Oku Onuora later extended that definition to cover all kinds of musical backing, so that dub poetry would include any type of music-influenced poetry (Morris 1997).

Michael A. Bucknor, quoting an article by Jeremy Morley, opines that the 1968 Rodney Riots (named after the Guyanese academic Walter Rodney) seem to be a plausible point of departure for dub poetry as these riots were as much about cultural independence and the refusal of British norms as about economic and social issues (Bucknor 2011).Walter Rodney was a former UWI student from Guyana who had completed a PhD thesis on the history of the Upper Guina in the 17th and 18th centuries.

After spending a year in Tanzania, Rodney had returned to the Caribbean and had become a lecturer in history on the Mona campus. Rodney became very popular with students and began to deliver a series of lectures on African history. He also gave talks on Black Power and addressed not only university students but also the poor and the unemployed in Kingston. In addition he held talks with the Rastafarians and these gatherings later spawned a book entitled *The Groundings with my Brothers* (1969).

The Jamaican government saw Rodney as a menace to society and in October 1968, they asked the Vice-Chancellor of the University of the West Indies to dismiss him. The Vice-Chancellor refused to do so, and the government later seized the opportunity to prevent Rodney from coming back to Jamaica after attending a conference in Canada. When Rodney's plane landed on 15 October 1968, he was served with an expulsion order.

The news of Rodney's expulsion soon reached Mona and, on the following day, the students staged a demonstration and decided to march on the offices of the Minister of Home Affairs. The students were soon stopped by the police who used batons and tear gas to break up the demonstration. The students went back to Mona, but their demonstration had been joined by a large crowd of Rastafarians, unemployed youths and workers, who started looting property in Kingston's commercial district.

The riots were quickly suppressed and order was restored a few days later, but these riots stand as an important moment in the history of the post-independence Caribbean because they showed that issues of cultural legitimacy were bound up with the dire social and economic conditions the islands were still trapped in.

In the 1970s dub poetry developed in Jamaica thanks to poets like Oku Onuora, Mutabaruka and the late Michael Smith, and in England due to the work of Linton Kwesi Johnson. The latter was to be particularly successful in his attempt to make this type of poetry popular with a European, multicultural audience thanks to his recordings, though he also used the printed word.

By the late 1970s and early 1980s, dub poetry was well-established as a form of "protest poetry" and as an offshoot of roots reggae which was mainly concerned with social and political themes like life in Jamaican slums, poverty, racial tension and economic exploitation.

Oku Onuora's "Pressure Drop" ((Brown and Mc Watt 281) and other canonical dub poems like Oku Onuora's "Reflection in Red", Michael Smith's "Mi Cyaan Believe It" or Mutabaruka's "White Sound" all focused on similar themes and were characterised by a certain declamatory delivery which seemed appropriate for "political poetry". This particular delivery was favoured in the early 1980s by Mutabaruka whose "White Sound" is concerned with the trauma of slavery.

In England, the Jamaican-born poet Linton Kwesi Johnson pioneered the genre and documented the plight of the Black British community in the 1970s in poems like "Five Nights of Bleeding", "Dread Beat and Blood", "Street 66", "Sonnys' Lettah" and "Inglan is a Bitch". Johnson published three collections of poetry between 1974 and 1980 (*Voices of the Living and the Dead*, *Dread Beat an' Blood*, and *Inglan is a Bitch*) and became famous for his accomplished reading of his own poetry in which reggae rhythms could distinctly be heard. As his Jamaican counterparts had done, Johnson used records and tapes to popularise dub poetry, and his recordings made him a household name in reggae circles. The four recordings issued between 1978 and 1984 (*Dread Beat an' Blood*, *Forces of Victory*, *Bass Culture*, and *Making History*) are all fine examples of Black British dub poetry and are primarily concerned with the situation of the Black British community in the 1970s. Poverty, racial discrimination, police brutality, sound systems, and reggae culture seem to have been Johnson's main preoccupations at the time and the poet even said that when he first started writing poetry he meant to use poetry as a vehicle for social and political protest (Johnson 2010).

In 1986 the first dub poetry anthology (*Dub Poetry: 19 Poets from England and Jamaica.* Neuestad, Michael Schwinn, 1986) appeared and was edited by the German critic Christian Habekost. This anthology included dub poets from England (Martin Glynn, Desmond Johnson, Linton Kwesi Johnson, Levi Tafari among others) and from Jamaica (Jean "Binta" Breeze, Mutabaruka, Okuonuora and Michael Smith) and Habekost's introduction replaced the poetry in its social and cultural context, paying particular attention to the reggae tradition of "toasting", or talking over a recorded track, developed by the deejays U-Roy, I-Roy and Big Youth in the early 1970s.

Habekost organised several "dub poetry tours" in the 1980s and by then Linton Kwesi Johnson was touring Europe regularly, invariably presented as a "reggae artist". In the 1980s most dub poets, except for Michael Smith who was murdered in Jamaica in 1983, continued to record albums and to tour internationally.

Apart from Jamaica and England, dub poetry also developed in Canada. As pointed out by Chrisitan Habekost, the development of dub poetry in Canada "is closely connected with Lillian Allen" (Habekost 33). Together with Clifton Joseph, Lillian Allen nurtured the art form in Canada.

Originally from Jamaica, she migrated to Canada in 1974 and settled in Toronto. In 1982 she published her first book, *Riddim An' Hardtimes*, and in 1986 her first album, *Revolutionary Tea Party*, won a Juno award. Two years later, her second album, *Conditions Critica*l, did the same. Allen also founded a dub poetry collective called De Dub Poets and they released an EP in 1983. Touring ceaselessly during the 1980s, she inspired other dub poets like Devon Haughton, Clifton Joseph, adhri zhina mandiela, Afua Cooper, and Klyde Broox.

Lillian Allen is also well-known for her quarrel with the League of Canadian Poets. Indeed in 1984 Allen and her dub poetry collective applied for membership of that prestigious league but their application was turned down because, according to the members, these dub poets were just "performers" and their poetry failed to satisfy the standards of the league. Although the dub poets' application was eventually accepted a couple of years later , the initial rejection did not bode well for the reception of dub poetry in academia.

By the mid-1980s, dub poetry seemed to be in crisis or at an impasse, as a number of dub poets like Jean "Binta" Breeze and Linton Kwesi Johnson began to voice their concern about the limited use of the label "dub poetry" and even claimed that dub poetry had become a mere gimmick or fashion.

In an interview granted to the journalist Dotun Adebayo and published in the Black British newspaper *The Voice* in 1989, the dub poet Jean Binta Breeze declared that she had to "get out of the confines of dub poetry...It was so restricting having to write poetry to a one-drop reggae rhythm. That can't be good for any poet I'm not screeching and shouting my poetry any more I've discovered that poetry is not synonymous with preaching" (Adebayo 1989, quoted in Habekost 1993)

Linton Kwesi Johnson had expressed similar views in an interview with the Jamaican critic and poet Mervyn Morris: "...eventually I found that I was getting drawn closer to the music and trying to write within the strict parameters of the reggae form which is very limiting. You're not conscious of it at the time, but you get drawn closer and closer and closer to the music until in the end what you're doing is basically writing reggae songs or composing reggae music" (Markham 260). This growing awareness that he was slowly turning into a reggae act led Linton Kwesi Johnson to put an end to his touring in the mid-1980s in order to concentrate on his writing.

These dub poets' reservations about the limitations of dub poetry were echoed by the stance taken by some academics who expressed concern about the literary quality of much dub poetry, and about the need to find a way to assess the quality of these poems.

In his review of Christian Habekost's *Dub Poetry: 19 Poets from England and Jamaica*, the Jamaican critic Victor Chang had written that with dub poetry "One cannot expect any subtlety of approach…registering a complexity of position or feeling" (Habekost 48). Chang had taken issue with Habekost's contention that dub poetry could only be appreciated by attending a dub poetry performance. This would have meant that the dub poets themselves would have had to mediate between their material and the audience. Chang also wrote that a lot of the poems in Habekost's anthology did not go beyond the "enraged shout" (Chang 49-52).

Around the same time, the British critic Stewart Brown published an article in the journal *Poetry Wales* in which he voiced similar concerns: " As dub poetry becomes a commercial product, as its performers, like Benjamin Zephaniah or Mutabaruka or Ras Levi Tafari, become media *stars* and strive to entertain a mass, multicultural audience, there seems to me a real danger that the protest, the anger, the fire becomes an act, while the image, the dub/rant/chant/dance becomes the real substance of the performance" (Brown 53-54).

Brown's reservations concerning the validity of dub poetry were echoed a few years later by the Guyanese critic Gordon Rohlehr in his introduction to *Voiceprint*, an anthology of oral poetry. Rohler wrote that "dub poetry is at its worst a tedious jabber to a monotonous rhythm" (Brown, Morris and Rohler 18). It must be said that this quote, taken out of context, is by no means representative of Rohlehr's view on dub poetry as he has always championed oral art forms and the oral tradition more generally. Indeed the words "at its worst" are proof that Rohlehr was not making a sweeping statement, but simply pointing out the worst excesses of the genre. That said, the fact that even a champion of oral art forms like Gordon Rohlehr could voice doubts about the validity of dub poetry shows that a debate was going on at the time on the quality of this type of poetry.

Traces of that debate can also be found in an article by Carolyn Cooper that was originally published in the journal *Wasafiri* and which was reprinted in her seminal study of Jamaican orality, *Noises in the Blood- Orality, Gender and the "Vulgar" Body of Jamaican Popular Culture.* The article was primarily about "the performance poetry of Jean Binta Breeze and Michael Smith", but also contained many insights about the reception of dub or performance poetry in England. Cooper insisted on the danger inherent in the commercialisation and commodification of the art form in a multicultural society like Britain where an "undiscriminating audience" might applaud as art "a noisy belch". Cooper had also quoted a few lines from a rap by Benjamin Zephaniah which, according to her, was "pure greeting-card doggerel" (Cooper 72).

This negative reception of dub poetry was countered by the German critic Christian Habekost who published his *Verbal Riddim: The Politics and Aesthetics of African-Jamaican Dub Poetry* in 1993 in which he remarked that "in Jamaica, the heartland of reggae and dub, the majority of academics have had serious reservations about the genre" (Habekost, 1993, 6).

Habekost championed dub and performance poetry and laid the emphasis on the cultural context in which dub poetry must be appreciated and on the performance element inherent in such an art form. Habekost found Breeze's and Linton Kwesi Johnson's criticisms unfair and unjustified, and praised Benjamin Zephaniah's poetry as the way forward. So there was a rift between the "true believers" and the sceptics, between those who advocate the cultural significance of dub poetry and those who admire only certain dub poets and point to the limitation of the genre as a *literary* form. This is the well-known opposition between high culture and popular culture, between real writers and "performers". Professor Mervyn Morris claims that Habekost is partly responsible for this problem on account of the poems he included in his 1986 anthology and because of his championing of Benjamin Zephaniah in his 1993 study of dub poetry (Morris 1997).

The debate over the literary merits of dub poetry gave rise to a new sub-genre which could be called self-referential dub poetry or "meta dub". The term "meta dub" was coined by Professor Carolyn Cooper in an article about the performance poetry of Jean Binta Breeze and Michael Smith (Cooper 68-87). Meta-dub poetry, or self-referential dub poetry, is a kind of self-reflexive poetry which tackles themes like the nature of dub poetry and the relationship between dub poets and their audience. These poems tend to address such concerns as the predictability of dub poetry, that is its reliance on a set of conventions that have come to define the genre. Mutabaruka's "Dis Poem"is a case in point (Brown and McWatt 120). In "The Angry Black Poet", Benjamin Zephaniah dealt with the issue of the commercialisation of dub poetry. The title of the poem echoes the well-known phrase "the angry young men" which was used to describe the work and attitude of a number of young writers who emerged in Britain in the 1950s like John Osborne

(Zephaniah *Too Black* 29).

Zephaniah dealt with the same theme in another piece entitled "Knowing Me" (Zephaniah *Too Black* 62). The line "I don't have an identity crisis" recurs throughout the poem and drives home the poet's message: he is not to be forced into the straightjacket of the protest tradition and begs to differ.

The Jamaican performance poet Mbala put dub poetry in historical perspective in his "History of Dub Poetry" (Dawes 133). In this poem, Mbala sets out to explain how dub poetry developed as an oral art form as an offshoot of the African oral tradition symbolised by the griot as alternative newscaster, but Mbala's poem proposes a wider interpretation of the concept of dub poetry as it also refers to "di rapso man/ calypso man" who "sad yu/laaf yu/to tears dat melt weh yu walls". Dub poetry's function is to entertain and enlighten its audience and to uplift them ("dancehallin towards yu conscience").

Dub poets reacted to the criticisms levelled at their art form by focusing increasingly on the very nature of dub poetry and by pointing out some of its weaknesses, such as its predictability and the pitfall of commercialisation. These new developments are evidence that dub poetry is not moribund and can be a vehicle for intellectual debate. In other words, the dub poets can now assess their work critically. With such a new approach, dub poetry emerged as a sophisticated art form, as a vehicle for humour and parody. The protest mode was seen as one of the many voices available to dub poets today, but certainly not the only one.

As pointed out by Michael A. Bucknor, the publication of Christian Habekost's *Verbal Riddim* in 1993 and the controversy it triggered forced academics to come up with new methodological approaches and new concepts to study dub poetry. Dub poetry's reliance on various media (the printed word and performance) led to new approaches to the study of this art form, and new concepts appeared like

Gordon Rohlehr's "voiceprint" or Carolyn Cooper's "oraliterature" (Bucknor 2011). Likewise, Michael A. Bucknor himself developed the idea of a "body-memory poetics" (Bucknor 260), an approach which interprets the materiality of print dub poems as the visual expression of cultural traditions embodied in performance. Susan Gingell expanded Bucknor's approach by including "explanatory apparatuses" and "word/letter/font placements" among others (Bucknor 260). Some of these new approaches have tended to focus on the strategies used by dub poets to "textualize" rhythms and performances (Caridad 2004; Gingell 2005).

This inter-disciplinary approach was made possible by the various controversies around the value and the evaluation of dub poetry. As indicated by Bucknor, postmodernist criticism was applied to dub poetry by Peter Hitchcock and by Bucknor himself (Bucknor 2011). Feminist and Marxist approaches have been used too. So dub poetry more or less became established as a sub-genre or a branch of Caribbean poetry and gradually found its place in various courses on Caribbean literature all over the world.

Nevertheless, dub poetry has remained a controversial genre and its status today is still debated. In 2011 the Jamaican poet Kei Miller posted on his Facebook page an article entitled "A Smaller Sound, A Lesser Fury: A Eulogy for Dub Poetry" in which he claimed that dub poetry was a moribund art form which harked back to the revolutionary 1970s and did not mean much to the younger generation. Miller identified dub poetry as a mainly diasporic genre which flourished in Jamaican communities in Brixton and Handsworth but was no longer current in Jamaica. Miller seemed to argue that dub poetry's revolutionary stance and rhetoric no longer reflected the zeitgeist in Jamaica and that when his own generation tried its hand at it, it sounded awkward and contrived, in other words "a lesser fury". His article triggered a spirited response from the Jamaican-Canadian dub poet Klyde Broox who claimed that dub poetry was still alive and still had a role to play. The lively exchange between Broox and Miller proves that dub poetry can still nurture debate and contribute to a healthy discussion of its role, value and mode of assessment. That is positive. Still, what has been lacking is the poet's perspective on their art form.

In a way, the idea for this collection of interviews came out of this debate between Kei Miller and Klyde Broox about the status of dub poetry. I had been interviewing dub and performance poets for years and I thought that in these interviews lay a response to Miller's stance, and a much better one than I, a middle-aged, white academic, could provide.

The interviews which are collected in this book were conducted in Canada, England, Jamaica and the USA between 1999 and 2016 and they represent a journey into the world of dub and performance poetry from the poets' point of view. They provide a unique perspective on the art form from the point of view of its practitioners. Some of these interviews were conducted quite a few years ago but I believe that they contain enough durable information to be of value today. The general idea was not to present a portrait of dub poetry in 2017, but to try to get some dub poets' perspective on their art form.

The poets are not presented alphabetically, but rather thematically, with the pioneers of the genre coming first, the next generation and then the Black British performance poets, and lastly Mbala, who is sometimes considered as a dub poet but who has quite distanced himself from traditional dub poetry (see interview). It is hoped that such an approach will allow the reader to grasp the evolution of the genre from a dub-based approach towards a looser, broader type of performance poetry.

Overall, these interviews point to the complexity of the dub poetry community, with various stances being taken and various attitudes to dub poetry being defended, from Kokumo's militant stance to Mbala's more reflexive approach.

All these views and opinions seem to indicate that dub poetry is not a monolithic art form and that it is capable of harbouring different approaches.

OKU ONUROA

Oku Onuora (Orlando Wong) was born in 1952 in Jamaica and grew up in Franklin Town, a working-class area in Eastern Kingston. After robbing a post office in 1970, he was given a 15-year jail sentence, but was eventually released in 1977, partly because of the success of his poetry.

Onuora started writing in prison and had gradually made his name as a poet. In 1974 the prison authorities allowed him to read his poems accompanied by Cedric Brooks's band, the Light of Saba.

In 1977, his first collection of poems, *Echo* (Kingston: Sangster's, 1977) was published to great popular and critical acclaim, and his first recording, "Reflection in Red", soon followed.

His first LP, *Pressure Drop*, was released on the French Blue Moon label in 1985, which led to extensive touring in Europe and in the Caribbean. Since then, he has released several recordings, like *Buss Out* (1993) and *A Movement* (2013).

Oku Onuora is considered one of the founders of the dub poetry movement and, together with Mutabaruka, the late Mikey Smith and Linton Kwesi Johnson, he has inspired many other dub poets both in the Caribbean and in Europe.

The following interview was conducted at the very place where Oku Onuora and other dub poets studied in the 1970s.

Interview (15 August 2016, Jamaica School of Drama):

Interviewer: I'm not going to ask you the usual questions about dub poetry or about yourtself, because, quite frankly, your biography is well-known - like how you were jailed and then got out of jail thanks to the efforts of Professor Mervyn Morris and other academics.

Oku Onuora: Professor Mervyn Morris was the only UWI [University of the West Indies] academic. Barbara Gloudon a journalist and Leonie Forbes, an actress, you know, they were prominent. I'd be clear, you know, because I've been known to burn out academics because I believe they're a bunch of hypocrites. Mervyn Morris is a beautiful person. I don't fight against academia as such, because I coached my children to seek higher education and all of that stuff, but for the most part, I believe that academia are a bunch of sell-outs, you know. Most of them are not for the people. You are for the people or you are against the people.

I: In Jamaica?

Oku: Yes, in Jamaica and globally. All over the world, it's like that. They tend to reflect, you know, the ideas of the ruling class. But they've always been powerful in the people's struggle, you know. When people from academia, when professional people become a part of the movement, then it adds to it.

I: You were jailed for seven years and that's when you started writing poetry, or did you start before?

Oku: No, it was while in prison that I started to write serioulsy. Prior to that, I probably had written one or two poems, but I had never really like taken up writing.

I: When you started writing in prison, were you aware of the work being done by reggae deejays like U-Roy, I-Roy and Big Youth?

Oku: I was aware of them, but I was *influenced* by people like Bob Marley, Peter Tosh, Burning Spear. Even growing up, I was never seriously a deejay fan. I love deejay music, people like Big Youth, U-Roy. They are great. But for me Bob Marley is one of the greatest poets. People like Bob Marley, Peter Tosh and Burning Spear were the people who *influenced* me as a writer.

I: So, when you were jailed, you had already come under the influence of these people.

Oku: Yes! Because I was a young adult when I went to prison, but I had attended a number a dances, so I had a musical taste and preference.

I: In terms of Burning Spear, do you remember any particular song or album that you liked?

Oku: I love "Foggy Road"! It's simple, a repetition, I believe it's a masterpiece! And then "Marcus Garvey" is an excellent piece of work!

I: So you have coined the phrase "dub poetry". There's so much confusion...

Oku: Yes, there's so much confusion! Let me say it and I've said it more than once! There's no need to coin the phrase "dub poetry" because, prior to me using the phrase "dub poetry", we had the phrase "overdub", "dubbing", "dubplate"; and then the words "dub poetry" came about while I was in prison and I would come out in the morning and this brother realised that I was writing poetry and all of that and he would say "Come on! Dub a t'ing! Dub a piece of poem!" And I wanted to distinguish myself from the normal poetry! I wanted to distinguish myself from all these people, Miss Lou [Louise Bennett], Chaucer, Shakespeare. There's nothing wrong with Miss Lou, but I was doing something different than Miss Lou, you know. Miss Lou, she was using a lot of humour, she was using a folk rhythm. You know, I see Miss Lou as a folk poet rather than as anything else. And when I looked at what I was doing, I said to myself :" Wow, it's a process of dubbing". Because my aim and objective was, *is* to dub out some unconsciousness, and dub in some consciousness. I dub in the reggae rhythm into my poetry: the rhythm of my poetry is reggae. And other forms of music, jazz.

I: So, it's not limited to reggae...

Oku: No, it's a dubbing process. It is what makes it unlimited. And then, after I described what I was doing, someone pointed out that Linton had used the phrase. But, after that, I read the article, because I did not read the article prior to describing myself as a dub poet. Because it's a common thing in Jamaica Big Youth's *Reggae Give Them Dub*...For example, "dub your girl", like that slow wine on a woman, it's called "dubbing", "rub-a-dub style". So Linton had an article in *Race Today* where he was describing the deejays as dub poets and that's too much of a different thing! He had never used the phrase to describe poets as such. He was describing the deejays as dub poets. I didn't read that article until it was brought to my attention because we don't get *Race Today* here in Jamaica.

But I am a dub poet, I don't need to coin the phrase: I am the first Jamaican poet whether here or in Britain, to use that phrase to describe my poetry, not a deejay, 'cause I am not a deejay, a dub poet to be specific. In fact, Linton was introduced to I and I was introduced to Linton at the same time, by the same person, Mervyn Morris, and when he met Linton, he said to Linton ;" Wow, there's a brother in Jamaica, and you remind me of him, you do some similar kind of work". And then Mervyn came back from the UK and said: "Wow, I've met a brother by the name of Linton Kwesi Johnson...". And I can categorically and safely say that I did not hear Linton talk about dub poetry when I used the phrase. Using the phrase "dub" as a prefix is something common in Jamaica, you know, like "dub the boy!", meaning "beat the boy!"; "dub a girl", meaning wine on her; "dubplate". So dub poetry falls into place! 'Cause in Jamaica, dubbing is a must: we've always talked about dub since the days when we had the A side and the B side, which we called the "dub side".

I: How did you work with Mervyn Morris on your first collection, entitled *Echo*? Did you read the poems to him or give him a transcript?

Oku: I gave him a transcript and we selected from that. So Mervyn did not do any kind of editing, because if you know my Jamaican English, it's more akin to the phonetic spelling of the words.

I: So, Mervyn Morris did not have any input in terms of the orthography.

Oku: No, he'd make some suggestions here and there, but, no, what Mervyn actually did was to assist me in putting my first collection of poems, *Echo*, together and having it published. I met Mervyn via Leonie Forbes, a beautiful Jamaican actress, radio journalist and TV personality. At first, my poems were exposed to Barbara Gloudon. Barbara Gloudon is an excellent woman. At the time, she had a column in the *Saturday Star* and I always looked out for her piece. It was called "Stella" and is was written in the Jamaican language. It dealt with socio-political issues and I was eager to read that column because she was addressing socio-economical issues. So I communicated with her while I was in prison and I sent her my poems. The first time one of my poems appeared in a public paper was because of the influence of Barbara Gloudon. She had my work published in *The Gleaner*. At one time she became the first female editor of a major paper here in Jamaica. She has written several pieces for the Jamaican Pantomime. So she passed on my work to Leonie Forbes who passed it on to Mervyn Morris and when Mervyn got them Mervyn came to visit me and we talked about my work. What I love about Mervyn is that Mervyn did not try to alter or change my poems. He gave me some useful pointers, some suggestions, and he assisted me in selecting the poems for *Echo* and I took his suggestions. Mervyn did not come with any kind of academic air. He just came as a poet. In recent times, I'm realising why we are so similar, why Mervyn likes my work, because my work is concise. I write short poems. And Mervyn is like that: he writes very concise poems.

I: What kind of reception did *Echo* get in Jamaica?

Oku: *Echo* spent five weeks number one on the best-sellers' list in the *Sunday Gleaner.* In less than a year, it went through about three or four reprints. The Tom Redcam Library complained because when my book was placed on the shelves, people would borrow it and not return it. There were reports of people downtown pushing handcarts with copies of my book in their backpocket. It was extremely popular because it resonated with the Jamaican people. In 1976 I entered three poems in the literary segment of the Jamaica Festival Competition and the three poems received awards. In 1977 I entered three poems and I won three awards in three different categories. The judges in the literary competition who were judging these poems could recognise the reggae rhythm coming out of the poems. Because, to be truthful, I am a frustrated singer. I love to sing, but I don't have a singing voice, so I use my speaking voice. When I do a piece, I hear music in my head. So for instance when I did a piece on my debut album like "Thinking" and "Thinking" is dub, it's jazz! I was invited to the Angoulème Jazz Festival.

I: What about the experience of recording your first album, *Pressure Drop?* How did you hook up with all these musicians?

Oku: My first recording, "Reflection in Red", I did it with Steve Golding, excellent musician, guitarist extraordinaire. So I recruited Steve Golding and he actually selected the rest of the musicians. Cedric Im Brooks played percussion. Then I did "Dread Times", "What a Situashan" and " I a Tell".

By the time I did my debut album, I was well seasoned as a producer because I had already produced my work. I'm an independent producer, from my debut single to my debut album, because I 'm talking about self-reliance, and if you're talking about self-reliance and certain things, then you should walk the walk and talk the talk! That's what I believe in: your work should be an example of your ideology, what you talk about. So by the time I was ready to do my debut album, I was well seasoned as a producer, so I selected young musicians, very young musicians. These people were not known at the time but I selected them because I knew them personally and I knew what they were doing. For example, my bass player, Courtney Panton, when I first met him, he was a known percussionist. When I met him, he was playing percussion over by the Jamaica School of Dance and then after a while he started to play the bass. So when I was recruiting musicians for AK7, I was looking for young musicians to interpret the work I was doing as opposed to musicians who were set in their ways, brilliant nonetheless, but that time I said :"I want to use some fresh talent". So I started to look around: Courtney Panton, and he had a friend by the name of Hewlitt, a drummer. One of the guitarists was named Simon. I met Simon when he had just graduated from JC [Jamaica College]. He was familiar with my work and my wife used to teach him when he was at school. He was with a group of young musicians and Chinna [Earl Chinna Smith], Chinna is an awesome teacher, had all these musicians around him. So I knew Simon from that time and he'd always wanted to play with me. Hugh Pape is an awesome person and an awesome musician: he plays the saxophone, he plays the flute and I met him while I was attending the Jamaica School of Drama. He played the flute on "What a Situashan" and the saxophone and the flute on *Pressure Drop*. The only seasoned musician at the time was Ras Bonito, who played lead guitar. Carl, who played keyboard, was a young musician, but he was involved in theatre as an actor, but playing music also. These are seasoned musicians today. For example, Courtney Panton went on to play for Shaggy and he toured extensively. He has a band called New Kingston. Simon went on to play for a number of musicians. Carl isn't playing music any more; he actually teaches drama. Musa isnt playing music any more: he's more into producing for cable television.

I: One question about "Dread Times", one of your most powerful pieces. When you wrote that poem, what was going on in your head?

Oku: All poems on *Pressure Drop* came from my debut collection, *Echo*. Generally, the poems from *Echo* reflect the conditions that lead the youths to prison, and "Dread Times" was written at that time when we were going through some serious economical problems in Jamaica. It's an echo from what I heard. It was like a daily occurrence in the life of the average Jamaican.

I: The poem entitled "Decolonisation", with its djembe drumming, reminds me of what the Last Poets were doing in the early 1970s.

Oku: Actually, that piece was not slated for recording. While I was in the studio working on *Pressure Drop*, I was informed by the guard (I was doing this at Tuff Gong Studios) that there was someone there to see me. His name was Olumede and he was from America. When he came in, I realised he's a friend of someone I knew from New York who has an African drumming and dance group. So Olumede heard that I was recording an album and he actually came to Jamaica *on his own*, and he said to me: "Oku Onuora I'd like to play on your album" and I said: "Wow! We are recording and everything's slated...", but then from this brethren travelling so far and his desire to be on my album, I said to him that we would record something on the next day. So he went away, and this poem came to me: "Decolonisation" and I thought : "Lemme read this poem on this riddim". So when he came in, I said: "There's a poem I 'd like both of us to do". So he listened to the poem once and then he started to play. So that was the first poem we recorded that night. And this is what I believe in, to this very day: it's still relevant, even more relevant than before, especially at this time of the year, you know, it comes to mind. We talk about independence, but getting a flag and an anthem from the British colonialists doesn't make us really free.

I: Your poem entitled "I Write About" came out of a confrontation with the prison authorities...

Oku: Yes, for the second time, my poetry was confiscated by the prison authorities and I was summoned to the Superintendent's office and he said to me: "Why you write so much poems about blood?" and I said: "Well, it's just inspiration...". So I went to my cell and that night the poem came.

I: I understand you met Michael Smith at the Jamaica School of Drama.

Oku: The first time I met Michael Smith was at the Tom Redcam Library, when I did my first public reading and he approached me and said: "I write poetry" and I said to him: "You can visit me at the Fort Augustus prison", 'cause at the time I was at the Fort Augustus prison and things were kinda relaxed: I could receive visitors. In fact, that's where I got my first typewriter from Judy Mowatt. Mervyn used to come there too. It was during a period when the prison authorities couldn't block me anymore; they had to work with me, because there were people on the outside rooting for me, people like Barbara Gloudon, Mervyn Morris So Mikey visited me and he showed me a version of "Mi Cyaan Believe It". Then we met again at the Jamaica School of Drama.

I: Was he already performing at the time?

Oku: He wasn't really performing at the time. He was writing. When I came from prison in 1977, I was in demand, because of what Mikey did, and the socialist movement, the democratic socialist movement was at its zenith. Michael Manley was in power and you had the Workers' Party of Jamaica and culture was being used by the socialist movement, like the PNP [People's National Party] Youth Movement. So the socialist movement was at its height and this is where Mikey and I continued our friendship. But we first met at the Tom Redcam library. Likewise I first met Linton in my audience. The first time I became aware of

Mutabaruka was in my audience. I did a reading once at the Creative Arts Centre at UWI and while I was reading there was this baby crying and people were like "Shhh!" This was Mutabaruka and his wife's baby, their first daughter, and she was crying. And I said: "No, let the child cry 'cause that's music to my ears!" And I said: "When I leave you to go back to hell it's gonna be weeping and wailing and gnashing of teeth, so this baby crying is music to my ears!". So the first time I met Mutabaruka he was in my audience. Mikey was at my first reading. I had never seen Linton perform before I started to perform.

I: There was a poet at the Drama School called Noel Walcott...

Oku: Yeah, man! Godfather Noel Walcott! We call him Godfather or Jahfather.

I: Whatever happened to him?

Oku: He's around, you know, he's not doing poetry that much. You know, I hear people talk about the "dub poetry movement" at the Drama School as if a movement started at the Drama School. It was no Drama School movement. It was developed while I was here, but I was always different in terms of my recording, *totally*, totally, totally different, but Michael Smith was awesome! For me, it was a pleasure to see Mikey, to hear Mikey, to perform with Mikey and we had this *synergy* , Mikey and I. I haven't seen anyone like Mikey today, you know.

I: Three years ago, you released a new album entitled *A Movement*, with Sly and Robbie, and Monty Alexander.

Oku: You know, *A Movement* for me was just an experimental album, because I revisited a number of my pieces that I had recorded before without music. I took poems that I had on my debut album and I put music to that. The album was only released on line, but a number of people are familiar with it in Jamaica. I didn't really promote it that much here in

Jamaica for a number of reasons, 'cause it was signalling my re-emergency 'cause I had taken a hiatus from the music scene because I didn't like what was actually taking place here in Jamaica. The music had changed a lot. And I didn't want to get involved. And even before that, the musical world, the progressive musical world of uplifting, conscious music was subverted: there was a subversion that took place, you know, because we had Margaret Thatcher, we had Ronald Reagan, and disco music became the trend. This is the era when Jamaican deejay music became prominent, during that time, because music plays an important role in influencing people's consciousness. Music is a powerful tool, is a powerful means of conveying sentiment, an ideology, telling a story. It transcends border, it transcends language. This is one of the reasons I decided to use music to reach out, because initially I saw myself as becoming an investigative journalist. When I was writing my poetry in hell, I did that to release energy, this pent-up anger, because I had escaped twice before, you know, and the second time I escaped, I was shot. Initially, I didn't see my self becoming a poet, a published poet or a recording poet. I saw myself becoming an investgative journalist. In fact, I started to do a course from ICS (International Correspondence School) in Creative Writing while I was in hell.

I: On that album, *A Movement*, you worked with a new dub poet called Jawara Ellis.

Oku: Jawara is the son of Owen "Blacka" Ellis. The first time I actually met Blacka, we sat under that very same Tree of Life. Blacka at the time was a student at the Jamaica School of Drama. Blacka was one the original members of AK7: he played percussions, and he did vocals, harmony. On my debut tour with AK7, Blacka was there. So Jawara grew up on it. So I had put *A Movement* together, and his father visited me and he said he wanted me to listen to something. So I listened and I heard the intro to "Sketches" and the poem came up! It blew my mind! And I felt so honoured to have a young poet sample my work, to be inspired by my work. I had never done that before, and I decided it to use it on my album. So when Owen brought "Utter Sketches" to me, I realised the reason I was waiting was for this thing, because the album is called *A Movement*, and it speaks about the movement continuing and it also speaks about the movement from one generation to the next generation, a continuation. And my daughter has a piece on it called "Atomic", a poem she read at her mother's sending-off.

I: This leads us to the new generation of dub poets in Jamaica. What about the new dub poetry scene? Is it very strong?

Oku: Yeah, man,! It's strong! People like Jawara, people like Maker (a female dub poet), people like Sage, it's very strong. We have people like Ras Takura. We have Neeto Mix. Other people may not notice, but for me, it's very vibrant. When Mikey Smith was about, it was just Mikey Smith and a few other people. Now, poetry is bubbling in Jamaica, not necessarily dub poetry, but poetry, spoken word. Spoken word in Jamaica is really up and running right now.

I: Is Oku Onuora a happy man or an angry man?

Oku: Yeah man! I'm happy! I'm not angry. I get angry when I look around and I see the conditions that we're in, not just here in Jamaica, but internationally, I get very, very angry. But I don't stay angry. There's a lot of things for me to be happy about. I am blessed, I am thankful, grateful, because I am surrounded and loved by people from near and far. The world is a wonderful place; it's just the system and some people.

MUTABARUKA

Mutabaruka was born Allan Hope in 1952 in Jamaica and after school began to work for the Jamaica Telephone Company. He had been writing poems since he was a schoolboy and after sending poems to magazines like

Swing, he finally published his first book, *Outcry*, in 1973. Mutabaruka had also been performing his poems all over Jamaica by then. In 1976 *Sun and Moon* came out, followed by *First Poems* in 1980.

Up till then, Mutabaruka had reached his audience by performing his poems at various venues, or through the printed word. In 1980 Mutabaruka performed at a concert organised by Jimmy Cliff, the African Oneness Concert, and his peformance of a poem entitled "White Sound" went down very well. The guitarist Chinna Smith was there and thought that this poem should be recorded, and the Rastafarian elder Mortimer Planner agreed. This was the beginning of Muta's career as a recording artiste and the 45 rpm "Everytime A Ear de Soun" was released in 1980 on the High Times label. It went into the charts and turned Mutabaruka into a recording artist and contributed to boosting his popularity. The popularity of that single led Mutabaruka to record more poems and in 1983 the LP *Check It* was released, containing poems like "Whey Mi Belang", "Butta Pan Culture" and "A Watch Him a Watch Me". Other LPs followed, like *Outcry* in 1984, *The Mystery Unfolds*, in 1986, *Any Which Way Freedom* (1989), *Blakk wi Bla...K...K* (1991) and *Melanin Man* (1994). Since then Mutabaruka has been touring in Europe and America and has appeared in films and documentaries. Indeed in 1994 he starred in Haile Gerima's *Sankofa* and appeared in the documentary entitled *The Land of Look Behind.*

Mutabaruka also began to host a radio programme on Irie FM in 1993 called "The Cutting Edge", which is a kind of free-form talk-show during which any listener, from any walk of life, can say what they have to say and engage Muta in conversation. The conversations often take the form of lengthy "reasoning" sessions during which Muta patiently listens to everyone's point of view and gives his own views on many topics. The programme has become extremely popular over the years and has kept many Jamaicans up till late.

Mutabaruka has built a powerful reputation over the years as a dynamic performer and as a charismatic orator/poet whose "raps" between the poems are at least as interesting as the poems themselves.

Interview (26 August 2008, Kingston):

I: When did you first become interested in poetry? What drove you to write?

Mutabaruka: Well, what drove me to write was, like, schoodays, my teacher actually. It was my teacher who gave a poetry work to do, and I actually wrote a poem, and she told me to read it in front of the class. It came out quite good, you know. In those days, it was like the Black Power era. Marcus Garvey Junior was my teacher. He had an organisation that published a magazine. So we started to put poems in that magazine, and then there was another big magazine named *Swing* magazine, and we actually sent poems to that magazine. And then eventually they asked to put the poems in a little book just called *Outcry*. So that started to make me feel that poetry can be something. So we started to recite the poems all over the place, and eventually recorded it. So it was out of a school class work that gave me that feeling, you know, that I can write.

I : Why poetry? Had you tried to write novels, short stories?

M: Well, I actually wrote a play, and five years ago I wrote an opera, which is sort of being worked on in England. The poetry is how I express meself in terms of how I feel, my philosophy and my worldview. I think it helps to put my mind and my perspective in a particular frame. I can write straight, you know, like a composition So the poems help to focus my world view and my feelings about certain things, social, political, religious.

I: And then there is the matter of the dub poet label which you're not comfortable with, as you've said in the past. So basically you're happy being defined as a poet.

M: Just a poet yes, because, you know, dub is not in, but the poet is still in. Because originally, I think it was Linton [Kwesi Johnson] who said that he saw the deejays at the time like Big Youth, U-Roy So the dub was the genre of music that was popular. It was like a version to the tune; on the flipside there was the version. So the engineer was the chief architect of a dub riddim. So the deejay rhymed over that dub. But for the dub poet the poems he writes are not necessarily focused on rhythms, but on contents. It's not the music that's pushing the poem, it's what he's saying. So the dub poet is more focused on what's being said rather than on what the rhythm is doing, as opposed to the deejay, who is also a poet, but the deejay is concerned with rhyming. So he's contented with moving to the beat. With the poet, the beat is moving to his words. The first move of the poet is the word. The first move of the deejay is the riddim. So the poet tends to be more socially, politically aware of certain situations and the music frames it in a way that is not necessarily rhythamatic. I can be rhythamatic. We can go on rhythms and move to the rhythm and ride poems to the rhythm, but, as I said, most of the time, the poems are written *before* the rhythm.

I: How did you make the move from being a page-poet to being a recording artiste?

M: What happened was that, in the 1980s, Jimmy Cliff did a concert where he lived. I was just a poet reading poems and Mortimer Planno, he heard me reading poems and he suggested that I should be on that show. So I went with

Jimmy Cliff's band and I rehearsed that poem, "Everytime I Hear the Sound". I rehearsed it with that band and then I went on stage and did it, and it was a total success. So I came back to Kingston, and Earl Chinna Smith, who was a leader for the band, he had a record company named High Times, and then I went to him, and he recorded the poem. And it went up to the charts. It was the first dub poem to enter the pop charts in Jamaica. And then that propelled me as an artiste, as a reggae artiste, because after that poem, we did an album named *Check It*. We came out of Jamaica, we went to Cuba with Jimmy Cliff, and then after that we went to California. And outta that California show came touring; I started to tour, I went to Nigeria the year next. I started to tour America. That aided to shape it. That tune "Everytime I Hear De Sound" was my first published recording. I did record a poem before, but it wasn't released. It was called "Where Me Belong". That poem was produced by a brethren named Errol Thompson and it was arranged by a sister named Enright. She was a guitarist with a band named Truth, Larry McDonald's band, the percussionist who used to play with Taj Mahal and Gil Scott-Heron. I did that poem in Harry J's studio. That was my first recording in a studio. But this "Everytime I Hear De Sound" was what propelled me as a recording artiste.

I: The first poem in the *First Poems* collection is a piece entitled "Call Me No Poet or Nothing Like That". Well, what's wrong with the word "poet", or what was wrong with that word when you wrote that poem?

M: What happened was that I grew up in a situation where I did not know of any Caribbean poet. When I went to school I did not know that Caribbean people write poetry, because most of the poems that I know were from Shakespeare, Keats, Chaucer, Milton and these poets. So I rejected that because, you know, that is not connecting. I related poetry to Keats, Milton, Chaucer, and I would say that what I'm writing is not necessarily poetry because I did not go and study what is the basic way to write poems. My poems were just an expression of what I think and what I believe in. So, in writing that poem, "Call Me No Poet or Nothing Like That", is just to rebel against poetry as it was seen in the context of English literature. The English literature poetry was what we know: I didn't have anything else. We had Miss Lou [Louise Bennett] but nobody saw Miss Lou as a poet. She was seen as a folklorist, a comedian, but she was really a poet. So it was really a rejection of de British idea of poetry. Why should I write poems about flowers, birds, and all these things? So we didn't know anything about Caribbean literature. I never grew up studying Caribbean literature.

I: Another of your poems in that early collection is entitled "Nursery Rhyme Lament".

M: Oh yeah, that's a social commentary based on what we learn in school. Again, those nursery rhymes were not called poetry. They were called "nursery rhymes". So in school we know them, we never really studied them. Every child in Jamaica just had to heartically know them. You never ever get a homework to go home and study a nursery rhyme: you just automatically know it. When we began to know them and becoming more conscious and aware of the stupidity, not the stupidity, but not understanding the connection they had with *our* reality, 'ca maybe the guy who was writing it knew the idea that he had in his mind, but we didn't, we just knew it as a nursery rhyme. So when I started to understand, getting conscious and everything, I said "What kind of stupidness are these people teaching us?" without explaining what it is all about. We were able to just say it, off the tip of our tongue. It was just a take off these things to say: "this is our reality. You know cow jump over the moon long time before man go to the moon". So all these other things, this is my reality, you know, Beverley Hills, as opposed to the illusion of the nursery rhymes.

I: There are three poems in the *First Poems* collection which constitute a kind of trilogy about Afro-Caribbean cults:

"Revive", "Retrieve", and "Reconcile".

M: Well, that is me now going into retentions, you see. In that book you can see we started to get aware and conscious of certain other things outside of my normal education. So this Kumina, the ground vibrate, these things were memories that was when I was with me grandmother. I remember these places me and my grandmother used to go, and I'm starting to reflect on it now. This was part of the African rententiveness of it. So "hear the drumbeats echoing through the trees", you know. All of these things is memories of when I was with my grandmother, and now becoming a part of that "drumbeat echoing through the trees".

I: These poems are very different from poems such as "White Sound" or "It's Not Good to Stay inna White Man Country Too Long", which made you famous. I've read somewhere that "It's Not Good..." had been inspired by the plight of West Indian immigrants in Britain...

M: That poem was inspired by Linton Kwesi Johnson. He had a poem entitled "Inglan is a Bitch", and I'm saying to meself from Jamaica, he's from Clarendon actually, and I'm saying to meself, "If England is a bitch, why stay there?". So that was my answer to "Inglan is a Bitch".

I: And how did he react to that "answer"?

M: Well, him just say that dey know that! 'Ca I was interviewing him just the same way you're interviewing me now, and I tell him "Linton, you know seh that poem was written because you talk about England is a bitch...". Politically, he was a very strong political person in England. I am a Rasta, and him [was] a Communist, and I am saying "Our idea, Rastafari idea is Africa, repatriation". His idea is to stay in England and fight it out. Yeah, that poem was an answer to that.

I: It's a very powerful piece.

M: Well, it's the first poem that I did that branded me a racist, ironically, in America. But it inspired a lot of Africans in Europe to go back to Africa, 'ca I've been to Europe, and I've been to Africa, and a lot of youths there tell me that the first time they hear me say that poem in Germany or France, it made them think about dem country, and eventually end back to dem country. But in America, where people is not aware that Jamaica have a connection with England, when you say "white man country", Americans have the presumptiousness to say that America is a white man's country, and America is *not* a white man's country! It belongs to the Native Americans. So they take offence to it in America, mostly in America. But it carry me, you know. It helped to propel Mutabaruka the poet to show that this is a poet of a different thinking, that the political, Rastafari thinking is engrafted into the poetry, you know.

I: Another of your famous pieces is "Revolutionary Poets".

M: "Revolutionary Poets" is a reaction to the 1960s. Eldridge Cleaver, Gil-Scott Heron, a lot of these revolutionaries left the revolution, and drugs out, like Jimmy Hendrix, Janis Joplin, drugs out. When I was coming up in the late 1960s, and I started to listen to these artists, they were very revolutionary, black or white, they were very revolutionary. Those were hippie days, the Black Panther movement, Eldridge Cleaver, a whole heap of them, drugs get them out, and Gil-Scott, he was the main one. When we look at their poetry, and what they were saying, and then look at their life, as a youth, when I started to become revolutionary, I said "But how dem people become that way?" And I started to reflect on Jamaica's situation, and I realised that a lot of leftists, Communists, dem was fighting against Marcus Garvey and Rasta. They were saying that Rasta is escapist. But when you look at the situation, is only Rastas leave, because most of these Marxists become a part of the system that is now seen as an oppressive system. So that poem was a reaction to that.

I: One of your poems, entitled "Dis Poem", is about the

relationship between the poet and the reader or listener.

M: Ironically, "Dis Poem" was just written in a way that I was just writing things, different aspects of the struggle, that I was confronted with, and I don't like to write long poems, I can't remember long poems. So I write "Dis Poem", trying to make a collage of different aspects of the struggle, and it was getting too long, and I thought "I can't write in that way, the poem will continue inna mi mind". So I ended it that way: "Dis poem will continue in your mind". It is me, it is actually me I'm talking to! I'm talking to meself. It's my mind I'm relating to. But I'm sending it out there because somebody have to be reading the poem. I'm surprised that a poem that I never really *thought* out, I never really *think* it out, has become one of my most popular poems. I've seen it remixed in House, Techno, I've seen it danced to by the National Dance Theatre Company, Rex Nettleford; I've seen it performed by different people all over the world. Some youth did it in House riddim, from Chicago, and it is my biggest-selling tune outside of Jamaica. What they did was to take the words and make a beat to it, and since then I've had about seven different remixes of "Dis Poem" by different people all over the world, Israel, Germany, England, America, South Africa, so much different remixes As I said, NDTC made a dance out of it without the music; that was something to see.

I: Now, "Dis Poem" reminds me of another of your poems which "continues in your mind" after you've stopped reading it. It's entitled "Siddung Pon de Wall a Watch Him a Watch Me". It's obviously about social issues, the two Jamaicas facing each other.

M: Yeah, it's a paranoid system in which poor people believe that everything rich people have was stolen from poor people, and rich people believe that everything *they* have, poor people want it. So there's a paranoia, schizophrenia happening in the society where I am watching you and he is watching me and no-one is getting anywhere, you know. It's a paranoia poem: who's watching who, where am I in the whole scheme of things.

I: Another of your poems was inspired by a well-known rock steady number by Prince Buster, "Judge Dread", and is entitled "The People's Court".

M: Yeah, that's my biggest-selling record in Jamaica. There's a Part I and a Part II, one about politicians and one about religion.

I: So, where does Prince Buster fit into the dub poetry scheme of things? Was he an inspiration? Because what he did in the 1960s in a way prefigured what the deejays and dub poets did later on...

M: No, no, what happened was that there was a tune in the 1960s named "Judge Dread" against the bad man-dem at the time. He was singing against the rude boys. "The People's Court" is the title of a court-on-TV programme. It's an American show where they show the courthouse with normal people, real-life courthouse. So the title comes from that programme. And then I'm remembering 'Judge Dread" when he was trying the rude boys, so I said I'll use that riddim to update it now and do the people's court and try the politicans. And it was so successful that in my thinking politics and religion is the main problems that we have. My thing was to go back into the studio and now talk about the religion, and about what religion is doing to the people. The two a dem was a hit. It was actually banned at the time in Jamaica.

I: Moving on to another aspect of your career. For 16 years now you've been hosting a very popular show on Irie FM called "The Cutting Edge". What led to start that show at the time?

M: Well, the radio station asked me to do a programme. I'm a collector of a whole heap of different music, so they wanted someone who could play reggae from around the world, different reggaes and African musical styles. So when I went there, inna my thinking, I couldn't just sit down for three hours and just play pure reggae and say nothing. So in playing the music I started to talk and eventually the talking become what was driving the show, rather than the music. So I started to talk and to give my opinion about Rasta, about politics, about anything, and it became a talk-show, rather than a music show. So it became the only show on that station that was not playing pure music, plus I introduced African music in the shwo, 'cause there was no programme in Jamaica that delved into African music. So I started to play African music, reggae music and poetry, and just talk. So eventually now the talking become the main thing because people started to respond to what I was saying.

I: So what are your objectives with this show? What are you trying to do? What is your ultimate goal?

M: My ultimate goal is to bring a certain perspective to the African mind inna Jamaica and the world, to recognise the African-centred perspective of themselves, to realise that Africa as we know it in school is not the Africa that is real, and we must be, like Marcus Garvey say, if you are more confident in yourself, you are twice more fitted in the race of life. What we try to do in all aspects of we life is through the art, through the daily living, through how we talk, through how we look, through how we perform, we try to bring that African-centred perspective to the people. So anywhere you go and you ask the people about Mutabaruka, they will tell you:"Bwai, dat bredren into African t'ing all right". We no eat certain things, we no wear certain clothes, and we is Rasta. And this was never proclaimed and publicly even on the radio, like we've been doing over the past 16 years. We're trying to show a perspective of Rastafari that is not necessarily heard on the radio in Jamaica. We bring a certain sensibility to Rastafari and a different kind of manifestation to Rastafari.So my intention is to really awaken the conscience and the consciousness of the people. What can I do to make people more aware of themselves and what dem supposed to do as African people inna Jamaica?

I: So you see yourself as some kind of educator, or a teacher.

M: Well I see myself as a person who lives a certain way and, if it can bring about a certain change, we say give thanks. We live we life a certain way, you know. When we talk, when we walk, when we speak, when we eat, when people look at we, we don't divert, we are not a artist and something else. What is my art is what is me; so I don't separate what I say in my poetry and how I live my life, and people *understand* that. From tha radio programme people realised that Mutabaruka on the radio programme and Mutabaruka walking down the street is the same Muta, you know. We don't change we language, change we wordsound fe suit the radio ear. The way we talk on the stage is the same we talk to people, so it's not like we putting on one t'ing here and doing a next t'ing here, so we try to make people aware that we can live a certain way and be who you want to be, and still be successful, still be who you are. You don't have to change to be somebody else to be who you is.

I: Over the years you must have had quite a few hostile reactions to the show...

M: Yeah, because we come 'pon the radio unapologetically and tell people "We no believe inna Jesus" and Jesus is really something *embedded* in the minds of the people inna Jamaica. So fe hear live upon the radio a man a-talk against this idea of Jesus is unheard of in Jamaica. So they invite we upon television programmes to defend weself and they invite theologians, scholars, but we still hold we own, so People don't like hear that. The youth-dem, it make di youth-dem t'ink, but if you are a old-time person, fe hear a man upon the radio a tell people "Bwai, right now, there never was a man named Jesus", it's a lot fe him fe consider that! When dem tell you about Africa and dem tings deh, is lie dem a tell, you know. Cause Egypt inna Africa, cause when I was a youth I never know that Egypt was in Africa, and if you go around and ask 'nough people, dem still no figure out seh So if you come pon di radio and really say these things, people call the radio station! In the early days, one Sunday morning, I was on the radio and I remember this t'ing kinda say "You cannot put a Bob Marley picture inna di houise and a Jesus picture" because he meant that Bob Marley was more important to him. Dem call the radio station and say "What kind of thing is that on a Sunday morning and you have somebody like that on the radio. But now people grow fe kind a respect the programme, 'cause, you know, it's the most popular programme on the radio at that time of the night. After sixteen years of having this programme, we can see it helped a lotta youths, because youths when we started out used to go a school, and dem just come back now and dem say when dey was at school dey used to listen when dem a do the homework and it helped dem through dem time.

I: There's another side of your career: after Muta the dub poet, Muta the radio show host, there is Muta the record producer. In the 1980s you were involved in two projects which consisted in recording dub poets and women poets: *Woman Talk* and *Word Sound and Power*.

M: Yes, that was Heartbeat Records. I was the first person that carried Jean Breeze to the studio. In those days I was with that company named Heartbeat and the poetry was more live at that time. The record company actually asked me to produce a album with poets. So they gave me the money to do it, so I did it. So it was the *Word Sound and Power*, and it was very good, so they came back again and I did this *Woman Talk* album that included Miss Lou on it. She did "Dutty Tough" and "Colour Bar". And I tell her "You know, you are the first dub poet!" and she was really pleased tha ta youth like me could carry her to the studio and *recognise* her work Cause she had heard about Mutabaruka but to know that Mutabaruka could recognise her work and carry her to the studio with young musicians and she ride the riddim wicked! She ride the riddim wicked, man!

I: Yes, the late Mikey Smith said that Miss Lou was the godmother of dub poetry! A few years ago, you were involved in another project which consisted in recording reggae artists this time, *The Gathering of the Spirits.*

M: Oh yeah, with Joseph Hill, Big Youth, [The Mighty] Diamonds, Hortense Ellis. The record company, Shanachie, asked me to do it, so I went to these different artists and I wanted them to do specifically certain songs. It turned out quite well you know, 'cause we got big top musicians.

And then the one I did was "What about the land?" based up on Chief Seattle. Some of the words were from Chief Seattle. This was the Chief who said "How can you buy what is not yours?" and if you decide that you will take the land, remember the trees, remember the rivers. So it was some of his words that I used on this poem.

CHERRY NATURAL

Cherry Natural is a Jamaican dub poet who has been writing and performing since 1979. Her first collection of poems, entitled *Come Meck We Reason* (Kingston: Careso/Volunteers Social Service), was published in 1989 and bore the influence of Oku Onuora's poetry. This collection contained poems such as "Come Meck We Reason", "Gold Chain Mentality", "Feel De Pessure", "Traces", "Question Dem" together with various sections with headings like "Exercise Tips", "Health Tips", "Intelligence Tests" and "Facts" which testified to the inherently social nature of her art. Indeed Cherry Natural considers herself as an "activist" (see interview) and views poetry as a means of making an impact on society.

In the late 1980s and throughout the 1990s Cherry Natural appeared regularly on radio shows and television programmes in Jamaica, which helped to establish her reputation as a performer. In 1999 her first CD, entitled *Earth Woman* (Virquarian Music Ltd), was released and her second collection of poems, *Earth Woman – Selected Poems 1989-2001*

(Bloomington, Indiana: Rastazumska

Productions, 2003) was published in 2003 by the American academic John D. Galuska, who wrote his PhD thesis on Jamaican dub poetry. More recently, a second CD was released, entitled *Memoirs of a Praying Mantis* (Kingston: Bamboo Media) featuring the poem "Send Di Poem Come" among others.

Cherry Natural has performed many times in the USA and appears regularly in Jamaica at various events, conducting workshops or reading her poems, sometimes with a reggae band. She has been nominated five times for the Jamaica Federation of Music Award (JAMI) and has won it twice.

She perfoms at various poetry festivals, in Jamaica and abroad such as the Chicago World Music Festival. She is a martial arts instructor (karate black belt) and has conducted self-defence workshops for women in the Caribbean, Canada, the United Kingdom and the USA.

Natural's poetry is an offshoot of the Jamaican dub poetry tradition, but with a feminist twist. Her 2003 collection is divided into three sections which give a fairly good idea of the main themes developed in the poems: "Tribute to My Sistas", "Self-Love" and "Revolutionary Soldiers".

In the first section, her best-known poem in Jamaica is probably "Earth Woman", a piece which is a paean to the black mother or to black women as "earth women" and revolutionary freedom fighters. "Be Yu" (*Earth Woman*, 13) has proved very popular too with its radical message of self-determination. The poem entitled "Pickney Poems"(*Earth Woman* 21) celebrates the link between creativity and womanhood and is about the relationship between life and art, about the creative process.

Cherry Natural sees herself as a revolutionary poet, and to her, art is part of the revolution. To her, poetry is a living art form which is embodied by the Jamaican oral tradition and which cannot be bound in books. In "Send Di Poem Come", she warns that her language is "no Anglo-Saxon English" and that the words she uses will not be found "inna Oxford or Webster". She claims that poems should not be "lock up inna book" but should do the work they are supposed to do by being performed. In "Word Soldiers", she celebrates the Caribbean oral tradition and namechecks or mentions virtually every important performance poetry practitioner, thus taking part in the Caribbean tradition of "naming" or calling the ancestors back to life.

Many poems take the form of dramatic monologues or observations on life spoken by a Jamaican persona, usually in Creole. Many pieces deal with social issues and provide a feminist and anti-colonial take on things, but the two often merge. Trimeters, tetrameters and a certain declamatory style place her poetry firmly in the classic dub poetry tradition developed by Oku Onuora and Mutabaruka in the 1970s and 1980s. The poem entitled "I'm Walkin' Out of Your Jail Tonight" (*Earth Woman* 44) was written for Emancipation Day in August 1997 and is in standard English, proof that radical dub poetry need not be in Creole.

Social and cultural themes abound in her poetry, as shown by the poems "Pressure in Di Home", "Senseless Killing", "Harlem", "Natty", "Fia Bun" and "Jah Guide". As a Rastawoman, the poet has written several pieces on the theme of social responsibility and on the need to project a different image of the Rastafarian movement. For instance, the poem entitled "Fia Bun" addresses the issue of the violence contained in the lyrics of many reggae songs by artistes like Capleton or Anthony B. In the 1990s following the success of Anthony B's "Fire Pon Rome", a string of songs was released on the same themes, with apocalyptic imagery and repeated calls to burn down "Rome". Natural pointed out the fact that this approach had become a mere fad or fashion.

Interview (Kingston, Jamaica, 28 August 2010):

Interviewer: When did you first get interested in poetry?

Cherry Natural: At school. I was a fan of Louise Bennett Coverley and Claude McKay. That was my transition to poetry. The teacher in the literature class gave the students a Claude McKay poem to study, "If We Must Die", and up to now, it has never gone out of my head. Louise Bennett used to be very much into the schools among my peers. I was the one who could translate her poetry very clearly out to the whole class. So the class would look to me to perform some of her works and I really liked what she was dealing with, y'know. And then listening to Bob Marley in the later years, I could see the significance of his poetry. I was mostly into the lyrical content of what he was saying. So this is where my transition into being a poet comes about.

I: Why did Louise Bennett's poetry need translating?

CN: Because it was written in Jamaican Creole. A lot of students could speak it. However they did not know how to read it. I was good at taking it from the page to the stage.

I: What about Louise Bennett? How did you become aware of her work?

CN: Through school and among friends and watching her on the TV. She was on a programme on TV called "Ring Ding". I was also aware of her from pantomimes. We used to go to some plays and things like that.

I: What sort of time period are we talking about here? How widespread was it amongst school girls to go to plays and pantos?

CN: I am speaking about the mid 70's. It was very popular as it was a part of our Independence celebrations.

I: What about people like Mutabaruka and other dub poets?

CN: Well, I didn't know of Muta that time, not at that time.

I'm talking about pretty, pretty young and later on, when I become an adult, I started writing because of Miss Lou. When I leave school now, and then I read an article about Muta and during festivals, a lot of the participants used to perform Oku Onuora's poems, so I know about them later, but I had already started writing. But my main influence was Louise Bennett. This was in the 1980's. Oku's poetry used to be performed during our independence celebrations.

I: What did you like about Miss Lou's poems? Her sense of humour, the language?

CN: The social commentary and she advocated for the use of the language and said we should use it. And we can say a lot of things like "Take kin-teeth and cova heart button". You use proverbs and it means so much, it can have so many different meanings.

I: What did you like about the proverbs? Why are they important?

CN: They were short and to the point statements. They are important because it was a way of passing down cultural values.

I: What are the poems by Louise Bennett that influenced you?

CN: "Dutty Tough", "Love Letter", "Colonization in Reverse".

I: She wrote about women as well, you know, the "Jamaican woman"

CN: No; I never connected to that aspect. I connected to the social commentary. During that time it wasn't a lot of people speaking out.

I: What kind of social commentary? Who were the people speaking out at the time?

CN: Commentary about race, class and gender. Some of the people were Burning Spear, Louise Bennett, Peter Tosh and Bob Marley.

I: From what I've read about you, you're often mentioned as a feminist poet. Do you see poetry as a vehicle for that?

CN: Yes, in terms of how I presented it. I see it as a very good channel. I'm an activist.

I: What does it mean exactly to be an activist poet?

CN: It means transporting your value system using poetry as the vehicle.

I: Do you see yourself as a dub poet, a performance poet, or just a poet?

CN: I see myself as a dub poet, a performance poet, a poet, *whatever* title. I don't mind because all of them have truth to it that connects to *me*. All of them connect. It's connected to the truth. I don't have a hard and fast rule like "I want to be called a dub poet instead of a poet".

I: Do you consider yourself as a feminist performance poet or as a performance poet who happens to be a feminist?

CN: I see myself as a performance poet who happens to be a feminist.

I: Why do you think it's important that women's voices are heard in poetry?

CN: It's important because our voices were suppressed for thousands of years. We did not have the privilege to use our minds.

I: Who is the "Earth Mother"? What kind of role does she play in the Caribbean and more globally?

CN: She is the woman who is connected to nature and dares to be herself. She is important to me because I'm represented by her. She plays the role of a muse.

I: Do you work with musicians?

CN: Yes, I work with musicians, not most of the time, but especially when I'm doing recordings.

I: What kind of musicians?

CN: Most of the times, it's local musicians. Sometimes it's collaborative and sometimes they are hired by the producer.

I: Do you prefer working with musicians or on your own?

CN: To be honest, I prefer just my voice unless I have a set of musicians that is connected to *me* and my whole way of presentation and can synchronise the poetry with the music. Most of the time when I go on shows and have to work with musicians, is musicians that is maybe backing a lot of artists, so they don't have time to *connect*, y'know. It's hard to work with them because they're in a rush, and as a poet, it has to be very *spiritual*, knowing that it's the music complementing the poetry, not the poetry complementing the music.

I: A few years ago, I read an article about you taking part in a programme in an American university, I think it was in Indiana. Can you tell me how it came about?

CN: There's a brother by the name of John Galuska. He was doing some research for a degree. He was here in Jamaica studying poetry. So what happened is that he connected to some of the poets but he didn't know who the females were. So everybody led him towards me. So he came to interview me and he started to get very interested in my work. One of the times I had a little school thing going, I organised a little group going into the schools. He came on one of them and I said to him: "You could do something like this in the States". He said that was a good idea and he would put the proposal to his college. He did put the proposal to them and he called me, saying he had got some funding and he was gonna bring me up. So it was myself, Mbala and another brother called Tommy Ricketts. So that's how it came about.

I: So how did it go?

CN: It was beautiful! And what happened from then, he came quite often and he started to study specifically my work and Mbala's work for his dissertation. He did it for the Master's and then he did it for the dissertation. So he spent ten years studying the work. So I've been there from Jamaica so often, approximately every two or three years.

I: Your first collection of poems, *Come Mek We Go Reason* (Kingston: Careso/Volunteers Social Service, 1989), was published in 1989. It contains poems in standard English and in patois. How do you make a decision to write in standard English and/or in patois?

CN: It's not a decision. I am a griot. So what happens is that I impart information from the ancestors. I am not somebody who just gets up and makes decisions pertaining to my artistic ability. I am guided by my ancestors. So it's like a woman giving birth: sometimes you have twins, sometimes you have triplets, sometimes you have a boy, sometimes you have a girl. At the beginning of the process, you don't get to decide what you have. So the poems came out like that. I give birth to different poems according to the vibrations from the ancestors.

I: Can you say more about those ancestors?

CN: It's just a vibration, stories passed down to us by our grandparents. So it's very cultural.

I: In 2003 your second collection, entitled *Earth Woman* (Bloomington, Indiana: Rastazumska Productions, 2003), was published. It contains the poem "I'm Walking Out of Your Jailhouse Tonight" which, I found out in a roundabout way, was performed by Mbala at the launch of your book.

CN: Mbala loves this poem and he's the one who chose to read it.

I: The poem entitled "Be You" is very powerful. It's a forceful poem. Can you tell me how you came to write this poem?

CN: At the time, I was writing a lot more revolutionary poems than love poems. I was just coming into Rastafari and the family was expecting you to function a certain way. And so the lines came up "They give you a costume, and it's not your size and you punish yourself to fit into it". Because what I was going through at the time What they wanted me to do, it felt like *pain*, like I was putting on something that don't *fit* me. So that's how the lines came up.

I: So it's not about women only, or about certain roles that women are expected to play It's a more general thing.

CN: Yes, it's a more general thing, like the type of career path and religion they want you to choose.

I: There is a poem in your first collection from 1989 entitled "Gold Chain Mentality", which to me seems to be very current. It could have been written yesterday.

CN: Yes, that one created a stir in Jamaica because they had a telephone thing and it was broadcast on the TV. Everytime you walked down the street, people would call "gold chain mentality!". My daughter performed that poem with me on stage. We did it together.

I: Why exactly did this poem cause a stir?

CN: At that particular time the people were into a lot of big jewelry, big chain and a lot of rings and were missing out on their true value so they would sacrifice food and medical care to buy this jewelry. I performed it with my daughter because it was a poem that she was passionate about. This took place at the National Arena. It was the Drug Awareness Concert. We do not perform as often as we used to.

I: Another powerful piece, this time from your second collection, is entitled "Send Di Poem Come".

CN: This one is criticizing the institutions, the so-called institutions who figure more or less that poetry must only be written in a certain way, 'cause a lot of poets, the only way you find them poems is by digging in some bookshelves or some bookshops. Dem lock up di poems inna book. *My* poems have to work: they are workers. Yes, I'll send them out to work. [Cherry performs "Send Di Poem Come"].

I: What kind of institutions are you referring to?

CN: Mainly the local universities and the churches.

I: Listening to you perform this poem, I was wondering how you managed to memorise a poem. Do you write it down first and memorise it later?

CN: Some poems you have to do a lot of drafts just to condense it, and then because it keeps flowing and it's not flowing properly, you do a lot of drafts and condense it. So what happens is tha doing a lot of drafts, it becomes like connected to memory. Some of them I have to memorise, but there are some poems that I perform regular, so I know these poems.

I: Concerning the writing process, do you write every day?

CN: I write every day. If I'm walking down the road and a line comes to me, I stop and write it down and if I don't have anything to write it on, I write it on my hand, or I take out a piece of paper and write it down, so that people sometimes think that I'm mad! Even in the middle of the night, I have to get up and write. The poetry is always running through my head. Yes, they use my head as a playing field, so they're always running through my head. So I have to release them on paper. There is a poem called "Pickney Poems" that Mbala loves very much. Muta loves it too. In fact Muta had produced a poem with me called "Fia Bun". That "Fia Bun" poem came out when Jamaica and the Rastas were burning fire on everything. So I was the first woman who answered back to it until all the other artists answered back. I'm the first woman who put a clarity to it and the poem got a whole heap of attention. Muta heard it and said he wanted to produce it, and he played it on his programme. So it was a phenomenal poem at the time.

I: Coming back now to the launch of your second collection at the Pegasus in 2004, Muta said on that day that to be legitimately accepted as a poet, the poems had to be in a book, which kind of contradicts your idea of poetry, which is to...

CN: to put it out, release the poems! Well, I do books, because the point is especially in Jamaica, you have to be practical in terms of people don't just take you and put you on a show. They don't see you as a popular art form that they pay you for your work. They might give you something but most of the time they want the poets to perform free, and you have to survive. How are gonna survive if this is what you do? Cause poetry for a poet is also a lifestyle. So that's why you do the books so that you can at least send some of the stuff and then what you can do is kind of get published more, because people don't take it and publish it like that. Maybe after you're dead!

I: Talking about being a working poet, do you work a lot with schools in Jamaica?

CN: I used to do a lot of that, but not recently. I've done a lot of workshops especially with women, with any unfortunate group like sex workers, women who get pregnant early, but sometimes you don't get paid.

I: Are these run as poetry workshops?

CN: Sometimes they are operated as poetry workshops and sometimes it's just dealing with the issues the poetry is addressing.

I: You're a Rastafarian. When did you first become aware of yourself as a Rastawoman?

CN: Well, approximately the 1970s, but I never start wearing locks until 1983, but it was in the early 1970s because I never used to process my hair. I used to just have it natural or plait it up, but it has never been processed. I was still going to school, I couldn't locks, but my lifestyle was more similar to Rasta, but even before I started wearing locks, they used to say: "A Rasta she a-turn!".

I: So in school you weren't allowed to locks your hair.

CN: No, but I used to plait it fine. So I had the tendency from very early, but I actually locksed from 1983.

I: What about your family? Did they accept the fact that you were turning to Rasta?

CN: What happened with my family is that, although they saw a tendency in me, I was a very conscious-oriented person, so I never do anything stupid, I don't smoke. I'm one of the Rastas who don't smoke. Two of my uncles had locks when I was a child and that created a lot of conflict because their whole lifestyle had changed. They started to smoke a lot, they started to colour the Bible red, green and gold, they started to put everything in red, green and gold and they started to refuse to have anything to do with Babylon or whatever they considered as Babylon. So it kinda created a conflict with my family because it seemed as if it's too extreme from reality. But I never did any of that: my whole consciousness was in my head and a different approach in terms of "Yeah, I am just a conscious person, but I know I have to live with reality". And because I was a very popular poet and they hear people talk about me, they realised that I'm doing a lot of things that make sense, because people talk about my work and the lyrical content of my work and I used to be on the TV quite regular and in the papers, in *The Gleaner* very regular. So they see that I am doing positive work. So after a while I could speak to even my grandmother, yeah, we could sit down and reason. Recently my grandmother died, this year, and my grandmother is a Seventh Day Adventist and in church they wanted somebody to represent the family, to speak, and everybody was pointing on me. Now there was a time when that could never be. A Rasta could never stand in a

Seventh Day Adventist church and speak for the family, but they pointed on me because of my clarity of knowledge and my whole view on life and the love that I bring with the Rastafarianism.

I: So you're telling me basically that things have changed for the Rastas in Jamaica...

CN: Not for *all* Rastas, no. It depends on who you are. Because, talking about the Seventh Day Adventist Church, maybe you might find a Rastaman who would go on the pulpit and, knowing that it's a Seventh Day Adventist church, he would say:"Rastafari mi seh, you know! Rasta live! Selassie I!" But I don't do that because it's *their* place of worship and I am tolerant in terms of respecting their boundaries. I speak on behalf of what they asked me too. I don't push my agenda. So I am accepted in my family now.

I: What might explain this change in attitudes to Rastas?

CN: Over a period of time, although they know we embrace a different form of spirituality, they realized that we are not a threat because it's dealing with love and integrity just the same.

I: Do you see your use of language as inspired by Rastafarian beliefs?

CN: I see my use of language inspired by the Rastafarians' language because of its close connection to natural living and identity.

I: Rastafarianism is sometimes seen as deeply patriarchal. How do you reconcile your poetry and activism with that aspect of Rastafarianism?

CN: I know it has that aspect to it, but because of my personal attachment to nature and feminism, my poetry is contributing to change. So it's not as it used to be .

I: What is the state of dub poetry today in Jamaica? Does it get much support from the government?

CN: Dub poetry was on the low in the late 1990's but now it's back in the forefront as a medium of social commentary. It does not get much support from the government at this time, but things are changing a bit and the future looks bright for dub poetry.

MALACHI D.SMITH

Malachi D Smith was born in Westmoreland, Jamaica and joined the Jamaican Constabulary Force in the mid-1970s. He was a founding member of the group Poets in Unity, started by Chris Bailey and Tomlin Ellis in the late 1970s at the Jamaica School of Drama. The group soon acquired a solid reputation as performers and appeared on the 1983 Heartbeat album *Word Sound 'Ave Power.* Malachi's poem "Victim" was featured on this album.

Malachi worked in Jamaica as a police officer and as a dub poet, an unusual combination, and he migrated to Florida in 1987, where he has continued to work in these two capacities.

Over the years he has released several CDs (*Throw Two Punch*, 1998; *The Blacker the Berry, The Sweeter the Cherry*, 2001; *Middle Passage*, 2003; *Luv Dub Fever*, 2008; *Hail to Jamaica,* 2010) on which he performs his poems to the accompaniment of reggae music or a cappella.

In 1998 his tribute to the late reggae singer Garnett Silk, "Psalm of Silk", appeared in Kwame Dawes' anthology of reggae poetry (*Wheel and Come Again: An Anthology of Reggae Poetry*, Leeds: Peepal Tree Press, 1998).

In 2003 Malachi won the International Dub Poets of the Year Award in Fort Lauderdale, Florida, and his presence in southern Florida as a dub poet is firmly established. Malachi has kept alive in Florida a tradition of performance poetry which goes back to Louise Bennett, one of his influences, and also to the dub poetry tradition in Jamaica. In 2009 Malachi headlined the International Dub Poetry Festival in Toronto.

Professor Mervyn Morris wrote in the liner notes to the *Luv Dub Fever* CD that Malachi's performance was "strong and subtle", and that his "speaking voice – his chanting on most tracks – played comfortably agains the various music rhythms and the discreetly enhacing background singers" (Mervyn Morris, liner notes to *Luv Dub Fever*).

The Jamaican poet Geoffrey Philp wrote that "Malachi's latest collection, *Hail to Jamaica*, combined nostalgia and social commentary in a distinctive voice that urges compassion for the downpressed. Ever a witness to injustice, an undercurrent of loss runs through many of these poems" (Geoffrey Philp, liner notes to *Hail to Jamaica*).

Malachi's latest CD, *Wiseman*, was released in 2017 and his latest book pof poems 'The Gathering' was published in 2018.

Interview (Miami, 27 July 2012)

Interviewer: I understand you were born in Westmoreland, the parish of Peter Tosh.

Malachi Smith: I was born in 1956 and my mum then and her husband were shopkeepers. My mum came one day and she was looking very serious, very stern, and she showered me and got me dressed, and had me pack my things. And the next thing I know I was in a truck. I was placed in a truck, which was the main mode of travel for country folks then, and I ended up travelling to Clarendon first (I was meeting my dad then) and from Clarendon I was sent to St Catherine, to my grandmother's where I ended up growing up. I also spent some time in Treasure Beach, where my dad is from. I spent a couple of years down there, but I finally settled in St Catherine.

I: Do you have any fond memories of those years?

MS: In Treasure Beach, I was on my own, missing my mum a lot. When I went to Clarendon, they thought I wasn't my dad's child. My older brother, he was much more light-skinned. On my dad's side, they're very light-skinned. And my stepmother's aunt didn't like me at all. She thought I was the devil; so she would beat the hell out of me. So it was like hell, living there until I went to my grandmother and of course she was very light-skinned too So I kind grew up through all of that, you know, and all of those things made me the person I am today.

I: When did you first become interested in poetry?

MS: It started very young, as a matter of fact, in St Catherine when I was at my grandmother's. She had a church in her yard, and whenever they had concerts at Christmas, I always ended up being the star. You know, I read nursery-rhyme poems and the whole place exploded and everybody would clap. And I remember one night, I was walking and I started singing: "We slaves, we slaves, hungry slaves..." and it started kicking, and then one year, the principal of the school told us they would be publishing this school magazine and so he encouraged the students to write poems, and suddenly I wrote three poems and they ended up being published in the magazine. So it actually came out of that and when this teacher, Mr Finley, asked me if I had ever heard of Claude McKay, and he lent me one of his books. All of that kind of fed into me yearning more to write poems.

I: What about Louise Bennett? Were you aware of her poetry at the time?

MS: Well, Miss Lou is my mother too! I always knew of her, I always admired her, but it was like from a distance. Moving to South Florida, I actually wrote this poem about her that I entered in a competition recently. When she came here, because she was in Canada, but she decided to buy a condo here and she would come down in the winter. So I performed on a benefit that these guys were doing for her. It went very well and her husband came and said : "You're a fantastic performer!" and he invited me to her house.So I went to the house and she told me how people had been trying to rip her off. I felt very sad about that. But one day in particular, something miraculous happened. I got there and she said :" Malachi, I feel I could eat a curry goat!". And I said "No problem, I'll get it!". And I drove away and I went and I got a big curry goat box dinner, and she said "Thanks Malachi, have some soup!". And that soup was so delicious, so rich, and after her passing, I kept on processing it, and it feel to me that she was passing on something to me in that soup, and Geoffrey [Philp] told me:"Malachi, you are so much stronger when you stick to dialect!", and I realised that that soup had more to it than just a little herb soup! And I wrote a poem for her last year. It's called "Thank you Miss Lou".

I: How did you hook up with Poets in Unity, Tomlin Ellis, Chris Bailey and all those guys?

MS: I had been writing by then for quite a while. I was a young cop in Montego Bay, I was doing a lot with youth clubs then before I joined the police force, I was fairly active with youth clubs. So when I became a police officer and when I went to Montego Bay, I got involved with the Montego Bay police youth club. Then I left Montego Bay and went to Lilliput and I started my own club from scratch. I wrote plays for them, I took them to competitions, we won gold medals, doing all kinds of stuff. I was living beside Bob Andy's manager at the time, and I met Bob Andy then, and Bob Andy said:"You're good! You should go ina studio!", 'cause I used to deejay! I was a very good deeejay then. So I decided that I was gonna apply for a transfer to go tour in the Community Relations branch of the Force so I could attend the School of Drama in Kingston. So I did get the transfer and I ended up in Half Way Tree and from Half Way Tree I went and did the exam for the Drama School, got accepted as a full-time student, but they wouldn't give me the study leave, so I went part-time. So, while there, it was a beehive of activity, and lots of things were happening there. It was the place where young intellectuals met to talk about philosophy. People from UWI would come down. It was a wonderful environment. Oku was there, Noël Walcott too. Mikey Smith was there too. Oku came up with this whole dub poetry idea. One day Tomlin said to me:"Malachi, since there are Oku and Mikey who are already well-known, we should start a little group", and we called it Poets in Unity.

I: When was that?

MS: That would have been 1977-78. In that time-frame. So it was Chris Bailey, Tomlin Ellis, me, Calvin Mitchell, Roy Rayon, the singer, and Clive Anderson, the actor. As we went along, we started doing workshops, and more people came on: Anita Stewart, Delroy Robinson, Paul Blake.

I: Did you perform on your own before you joined Poets in Unity?

MS: I did, I did. I used to do concerts. And while I was with Poets in Unity I got a lot of offers to perform as an individual, like Sting, they wanted me to perform. I said no, I couldn't, so we ended up doing a group project.

I: Did you perform at Sunsplash as well?

MS: No, we messed up big time! I think that was one of the biggest blunders the group made. As a matter of fact, a brother approached Tomlin Ellis and told him they wanted the group on Sunsplash. Tomlin wasn't comfortable with it and told them "No" before the group actually knew. I was away at the time. When I got back he told us that he didn't like the idea of performing between band changes and things like that. So every year after that we were on the list and were considered, but we never got back on it. I remember one year, Jean Breeze, who came on the scene *after* us, actually wanted us to perform in her set and the promoter said "No".

I: Your first single, from 1979, was entitled "Kimbo to

Kimbo".

MS: You know, growing up, I ended up in a love triangle. And one day I'm in class at the Drama School, and I'm always deejaying. So the guy who used to manage Inner Circle, Jacob Miller's band, said "You're always deejaying. You sound pretty good. Yo ushould go ina studio". So Kenny Lloyd, who was a promoter, and who used to produce Ini Kamoze, one day he came and said: " Malachi, we're going to the studio", Concert Studio. I think Ernie Smith had something to do with it.

I: The dub poem "Victim" was released as a single in 1983. Did you release other singles between 1979 and 1983?

MS: We were basically doing a lot of performances. In fact, a publisher, the person who published Muta, Paul Issa, he liked my poetry and he wanted to publish *me*. The group said "no", that it wouldn't be fair to publish me alone. It should be the group. So that didn't materialise and we kept on doing a lot of stage work and producer-owned shows. And after that I ended up hooking up with High Times, Muta's outfit. I ended up meeting up with them individually, and they liked my stuff, and I did quite a few shows in Jamaica with High Times. As a matter of fact, I remember vividly that one day there was a huge show that they did in Half Way Tree, with Jennifer Lara, Muta, Kiddus I, a bunch of reggae artists, and the show was dragging , and when I went on, the place lit up like fire! So we did a lot of stage work.

I: How did you end up recording for Heartbeat, which is an American company?

MS: Heartbeat decided to do a project. So they approached Oku, and Linton to produce this album. When they got to Jamaica, they asked somebody about dub poetry and stuff like that, and somehow Muta was brought, and Oku dropped out of the project. Linton came, but I remember the night we were recording at Tuff Gong, Linton didn't say a thing, he didn't get involved. So Muta ended up being the producer, but *initially*, it was supposed to be Oku and Linton. Straight up, most of us who are on the album to this day are very bitter about how it went. For one, it was never released in Jamaica. It was being sold all over the world. Muta said: "Jamaican people don't buy dub poetry. It wouldn't make any sense to release it in Jamaica". We couldn't see the rationale behind it up to this day, so it was basically like recording us and killing us, 'cause the people couldn't hear us. On the other hand, Muta went for the cover of the album that has a dictionary being burnt. It kind of played at two levels. The average person looked at it and in Jamaica we thought it was a Bible being burnt. So it kind of hit you slap in the face and people didn't really care for it. That album was never released in Jamaica.So at the time it could have opened doors with radio stations playing it, but people couldn't get the album! So it left a sour taste in our mouths.

I: What about the poem entitled "Victim"? What was the inspiration for that piece?

MS: At that time, there were a lot of things going on in terms of social conditions in Jamaica. I was also very much aware of the situation in South Africa with apartheid and stuff like that. So all kinds of things could have come into my headspace then, but basically it was a piece about the oppressed who find themselves in a situation and who want to do so much, but what can you do?

I: At the time, you were working as a police officer and you were performing as a dub poet. So how did you reconcile these two aspects of your life?

MS: I've always believed to this day that if you're gonna do something, be bold and strong and your detractors will run and hide. They will be afraid. If you're weak, feeble, they'll eat you. I remember two particular incidents. I remember I was working at the Criminal Intelligence Division then and someone came to me and said:"Whenever you perform, the tall, black gentleman that's always sitting in the front row, well he's watching you and tapes everything and stuff like that".

He was a Detective Sergeant. So one day I went to his office (they had a bureau or a special branch) and I asked for him, and he was shocked. So I said:"I've heard that you've been assigned to monitor me. Do you like my poetry?" He didn't say a word. I didn't see him again after that. One day, a Superintendent who had heard me do stuff at youth clubs, invited me to perform at this event at the police officers' club. So when I started to perform, they were all giving me bad eyes, and I kept on performing, and by the end of my performance, they were all standing and clapping. They realised that this work is no joke.

I: In 1987 you moved to Miami. Tell me about the reasons that led you to emigrate to Florida.

MS: A lot of things were happening. I'd been coming here for quite a while. But it reached a stage where one night, I was a homicide officer for Kingston-St Andrew, and I was driving to work. It started raining lightly and I looked across the other side of the highway and I could see this old man being chopped by some guy with a machete. So there I was on the other side of the highway; I couldn't run across. So all I could do to save him from being killed was fire a couple of shots in the air, which would give me the time to drive around and take him to the hospital. But when I started thinking about that night, my soul was on fire. There was this unease: "Do I want to continue living in a country where we've become such beasts, where we literally chop, tear each other to death?" I wrestled with it all night and in the morning, I went and said: "I want my leave". I decided it was time to move on. That's how it came about. I came here first on leave, and then I put in my resignation.

I: So coming to Florida in the 1980s, what was it like?

MS: The first time I came over, I was staying in a hotel downtown, and I walked around it seemed like I was lost. Then I found a bar, and it was all white men inside, there weren't much Spanish at the time, and there was this black girl on that stage dancing, like half-nude, semi-nude. I walked over to the jukebox, I felt angry and I saw one Bob Marley song and I punched it, and I turned it up, and she ran off stage! Then it changed with radio stations playing reggae music, you had nightclubs, you had a cool set of Jamaicans in North Miami Beach. Then it became more *comfortable.*

I: How long have you been working as a cop in Miami?

MS: Thirteen years.

I: Is it different from working as a police officer in Jamaica?

MS: All police departments have shades of each other. It is different in the sense that, in Jamaica, I knew cops who had never arrested anyone. Here is different: the society is predicated on numbers. "Show me what you can do, what you've been doing". So in that sense it's different. There's some admirable things about it. There's a whole arm that deals with community, youth events, there's a dynamics to it. You definitely need people to protect people out there.

I: What about working and performing as a dub poet in Miami? Do you find it easier? Are there more opportunities here in terms of venues, events?

MS: Here, it's kind of limited. There's a whole new generation, a whole new school called "spoken word" that is the in-thing. I have gone to quite a few of them and listened. You seldom hear a good piece of poetry and they all tend to sound the same. Occasionally you hear a piece of genius.

I: Is there a dub poetry scene?

MS: No. You have a few here and there. There's D-Merge in Fort Lauderdale trying something. There's Jagga.

I: On what occasions do you perform in Miami? Black History Month?

MS: No, I perform at huge venues. I performed at this Love-In Festival they had with Richie Havens. I performed at

Bayside, at the Broward Centre for the Performing Arts, at Centennial Park, at a Marley show. I've done quie a few big gigs here.

I: In 1998 you released a CD entitled *Throw Two Punch.* Tell me about the title-poem.

MS: Coming here, I began to think:"Why am I here? Working ten hours a day to survive when I could have a much easier life?" And then the poem came:"I came I saw, I conquered./ I trod this yah trod and I rocked this yah rock/ I really can't stop/ Can't put it down; got to keep on this struggle/Put up a good fight; have to do what is right/And throw two punch, throw two punch". Punch is actually a metaphor for hitting out at the system, against injustice.

I: In 2001 you released a CD entitled *The Blacker the Berry, the Sweeter the Cherry.*

MS: Well, the title-poem is a celebration of our Jamaican women. As a matter of fact, I ended up putting some tracks from *The Blacker the Berry* on the *Luv Dub Fever* CD, which is a more holistic CD and is dedicated and livicated to my sisters.

I: You wrote two poems about the reggae artists Garnett Silk ("Psalm of Silk") and Alton Ellis ("Let Him Try"). I found the one about Alton Ellis very moving.

MS: I respect my elders and like giving respect where respect is due. So here I am MCing a major concert at Centennial Park and Alton was on the show. Shinehead, the contemporary artist was there. And I noticed that the promoter's wife got this big fish dinner and she gave it to Shinehead and then I looked offstage and then I saw Alton Ellis standing in the sun with a ticket in his hand to get food. And I thought:"This can't be happening!". So I went down and I said: "Fada, just sit down" and I went and got him his food and drink.

I: I like you wove the titles of some of his songs into the poem.

MS: I read it in Colombia about two weeks ago. They loved it.

I: What about the one about Garnett Silk?

MS: I was freelancing with *The Gleaner* at the time when Garnett passed. So the Editor for Miami come and said:"Malachi, I'd like you to write a poem. Can you write a poem for Garnett?". So I wrote "Psalm of Silk" and it ended up being published in the overseas *Gleaner* and the Jamaican *Gleaner* published it.

I: You also wrote a poem entitled "My Jamaican Tongue", which is on your website. Do you always write in Creole or patois?

MS: I don't , I don't. I write in standard English too. However it comes back to Miss Lou and her influence. A number of factors, and specific incidences impacted on the writing on this poem. First and foremost, I dearly love my homeland and my Jamaican brothers and sisters. Secondly, I'm acutely aware of the significant part my Jamaican tongue played in our collective survival of the brutal system of slavery. This beautiful tongue was used as a weapon, a disguised mode to defeat our slave masters. Thirdly, being in the USA, persons are always asking me why you don't speak like an American. I always tell them the blunt truth. I'm very proud of whom I am and I proudly celebrate it daily with all the fibers of my being. During my undergraduate years at Florida International University (FIU), I found myself in this honours class discussing a piece of Southern literature. I listened to all the students attentively; however, when I started speaking I was ignored because of my "Jamaican tongue." I got pretty upset and I told the class I listened to their discourse and I demanded the same respect of them. They got the message. Then one day I was at work training a newly graduated female police officer. She asked me, "Why don't you speak like an American?" I demonstrated to her that I could and then I went right back to my tongue. I became close to Miss Lou when I moved to the USA, and this bonding, no doubt, came out sweetly in this piece.

I: In that poem, you mentioned Don Drummond. Why Don Drummond?

MS: Because he had that romantic type of feeling. It is sweet, it is curried, it does the jerk. So I used the simile "like Don Drummond's trombone."

I: You also mentioned "mento" in that poem.

MS: Because, growing up, you'd hear it. It was part of the early influence on the music. In the 1970s it was very popular; you had Stanley and the Turbines. He died a few years ago. They won the Popular Song Contest a couple of times with songs like "Leave Me Kiseeloo", "Healing in the Balmyard". It was like the Spanish marrying the African tradition and creating a unique type of rhythm.

I: On the *Middle Passage* CD (2003), there is a poem entitled "Question". It's a powerful piece about political violence in Jamaica.

MS: “Question” is a sarcastic poem about growing up in Jamaica and the bloodshed of the 70s and 80s when the USA and the then USSR were fighting for our turf, and guns overran the tranquility of our island. Guns everywhere. Killings everywhere. During that time, the makers of these weapons of destruction were enjoying mostly peace and tranquillity until the same guns returned to their streets.

I: On the same CD, there is a piece entitled "Pocomania Politics".

MS: “Pocomania Politics” is a reflection on the trivialisation of our political parties and particulary, politicians at home. One of our former Prime Ministers used to “jump poco” to endear himself to the masses. The art form itself is a great one, highly influenced by African traditions. But when Jamaican politicians get involved in things, it becomes merely a “poppy show” dance. The voice in this piece is saying "stop playing games with people. Wheel and come again".

I: What about "Mr President", which is on the same CD. Could you tell me more about this piece?

MS: This poem was written in the Ronald Regan era when blatant racism came back almost as the norm. I was saddened by it, because, despite how prominent blacks were in the US, and despite our historical and pioneering roles in many facets of the society, we were being treated otherwise. The poem said "enough is enough".

I: Your latest CD (2010) is entitled *Hail to Jamaica.*

MS: I thought that it was time to celebrate Jamaica. It sounds different from the others. The collection starts with the national anthem being recorded as a poem with a deliberate acoustic guitarist, Keith Stoddard. One day, I was on my way to Treasure Beach and on that day the sea had that sweet, rich blue.

I: There's a poem on your website entitled "Move Up".

MS: That poem was looking at my people and like saying:"Hey, you know, I hope that we're old enough now to start respecting each other's opinions, to find some common ground and take ourselves to the next level. So let's move up!". It is a reflective poem meant to call my Jamaican brothers and sisters into action of maturity in our opinions and behaviours towards each other. I’m very emotional about the state of affairs of my people. For the most part, we seem to lack maturity for differences of opinions and the holders of the instruments of power in the society use this reality to manipulate hungry-belly people into killing each other for the simplest thing. So the poem is a cry for unity, understanding, tolerance and respect of differences. The piece is one of my more recent pieces.

Interview update (May 2017):

I: You've been living in Miami since the late 1980s now. Tell me about the dub poetry scene or spoken word scene in Miami. In what way has it changed over the years?

MS: There isn't really an oficial dub poetry scene in South Florida. There are some Jamaican dub poets in Broward County that colloborated on a few projets, but nothing much is happening in terms of performances. On the other hand, the spoken word scene is going alone although not as popular as before. African-Americans usually dominate the spoken word scene. In terms of airplay and performances in South Florida, I'm usually it. There is Dr. Sue [Dr Susan Lycett Davis] who specializes in writing dialect, more or less in the same mode as Miss Lou.

I: You recently released a new CD (*Wiseman*). What do you hope to achieve with this CD?

MS: A lot. My most successful piece to date, in terms of airplay and appeal, is "How Yuh Mek Har Massa God" This poem was done on a popular rhythm which guaranteed it airplay. *Wiseman* is also done on a slew of popular rhythms. It is the type of album that should have broad appeal and enjoy support from the faithful and new converts. Because I have found myself in such a dead space for so long, it has inhibited my status, or at least I feel that way, in the eyes of the purists. I think this album is going to change that narrative. I believe it will excite persons at home and in the diaspora and maybe even an international audience to the potency of my work and voice.

I: What is the role of the dub poet today?

MS: I believe it has changed from the role of the storyteller telling the stories of his people. He/she is one who opens minds and eyes through education via his tool which is his/her words. The dub poet still has to be mission-oriented, must advocate for the oppressed and dispossed of earth, must paint and see for the blind, must speak for the tongueless, must dance for the danceless, must be an endless warrior against injustice, must be a healer, must be a trouble-maker, must be a peacemaker.

I: Do you regularly link up with other dub poets in Jamaica or elsewhere?

MS: I do. Every year I visit Jamaica and I usually read at the Poetry Society of Jamaica, an off-shoot that came out of my original group Poets in Unity, monthly fellowship at the Edna Manley College of the Arts.

I: What is the future of dub poetry?

MS: It is what we make it. I don't believe the principals are trying hard enough to market the artform. I believe dub poets have to create the environment to ensure more airplay as the genre is popular at the grassroots level but it needs to take a sizable slice of the media to become accepted. We also need to do more for each other. I believe some dub poets are selfish individuals who only care about themselves and don't give a damn about anyone else. As long as the money is right, that is all some care about. Difficulties with getting published has also impacted dub poetry negatively. With the release of *Wiseman* and the response it has been getting so far, dub poetry is alive and ready to kick down some fences.

KLYDE BROOX

Klyde Broox was born in Delveland, Jamaica and left high school to teach and perform as a poet. He won the Nathan Brissett Poetry Competition in 1978 and began to perform regularly in Jamaica. His first book, *Poemstorm*, was published in 1979. In 1992 he was granted a James Michener Fellowship to the University of Miami Caribbean Writers Summer Institute and in 1993 he migrated to Canada, settling in

Hamilton, Ontario. In the 1990s he was a member of Toronto's Dub Poets Collective. His collection of poems *My Best Friend is White* was published in 2005.

Interview (Toronto, 12 August 2015):

Interviewer: What is the function or value of dub poetry today?

Klyde Broox: We're using refrains, mnemonic devices because we're trying to dub a specific way of seeing the world onto the audience, and it works! Just Saturday night, I did a performance with mostly white people and after that we were talking like "Wow! This refrain thing is in my head", and the idea that's underneath that is soaking through into my consciousness, and that's very important. So to me dub is about the translocation of skills and I've worked with farmworkers in different languages, with workers So I am dubbing in the attitude as a performer and I've tried it to a limited extent in the workplace and they said to me: "This thing works!". Many working-class people told me: "Once I heard you guys, I stopped hating poetry!" You know, from the 1970s till now, dub is an organic form that versions itself like digital technology I do different versions of my poems, dubbing in something, dubbing out something else, and dub poetry began the spoken word movement in Canada. There was no spoken word before Lillian came and then to me groundbreaking work was "Dub Poets in a One-Poem Town". And the performance makes the poet a worker because what the challenge to me as a dub poet is this idea of the poet, the artist being in a separate class called the creative class, which gives you access to the working class, the upper class, the middle class because of your art, but then where are you, as an individual, located. As someone who was displaced from the teaching profession and came to Canada, after working in a factory, I realised that after you leave the factory, you don't take home the work like you do in teaching, so that gave me more time, in my head, to be a poet! And that's very important in my personal development because, you know it, a teacher never stops working!

I: I understand that both you and the dub poet Michael St George live in Hamilton.

KB: I'm very excited because we're using dub to start a movement now in Hamilton! Because Lillian told that a great surge in arts an culture happened in Toronto after 1993 and the dub poetry festival and we had the dub poetry festival in Hamilton in 2007, and now there's this huge arts and culture thing happening in Hamilton and transforming the community, from a steel town to a culture town and the fact that Michael and me live in the same building is significant. And Lillian has been giving talks at my events ansd she wants toset up a dub institute there.

I: A few years ago, the Jamaican poet Kei Miller posted an article on his Facebook page in which he claimed that dub poetry was associated with the 1970s and basically not really relevant today.

KB: My argument to Kei is that they're looking in the wrong place: they are looking for the anger, but what we're using dub to do now is anger management! I'm working on an idea I'm trying to sell the corporate world now, commercialising dub poetry. So the thing is you have to change your standard procedures at work or you have a new safety plan to install: you give that to a dub poet and he will make them into a poem with those mnemonic devices and you programme is in the heads of the workers and they have fun! That's the next level I want to take it because we have obvious skills. I'm also doing stuff with people in workshopping which is not about being a poet but about your public speaking skills, your projection and your diction. Also, the next level is what I call "discourse subversion", like you go into a room and someone makes a power statement. How do you pull the rug from under that power statement with your reply and let the person know that "Hey! We're on a level mental playing field here and no matter what your status is, physically, intellectually, you have to deal with me because of just that response!" That's the sort of thing we're doing.

I: In a recent article, the critic Michael A. Bucknor wrote that Bongo Jerry's "Mabrak" could be considered as one of the first dub poems.

KB: Back in 1992 at the Caribbean Writers Summer Seminar at the University of Miami, Kamau Brathwaite said to me :" You guys now have a playing field with the cursor and you can grab words! And you should start looking at how this cut and paste thing works in your dub field!" And Bongo Jerry's poem, "Mabrak", to me is the first dub poem! Orthography, fonts, this work he did in an analog field is what we're doing now with word processing. Because, Brathwaite and Miss Lou *and* Claude Mc Kay [were important too], because when you're circumscribe it like that, what you do is cutting off dub from its literary heritage and that is what the problem is with that academic reading. So my argument is that dub poets did not create dub poetry. Dub poetry created dub poets. Rastaman was the first dub poet. Bongo Jerry represents that. The Rastaman was the first person going around the community, the village doing exactly what the dub poet is doing now, the public intellectual, the shit disturber, undermining the narratives and discourses of Babylon. And I'm also arguing that all New World cultures are dub cultures because they're creole cultures and that this poetry came out of that.

YASUS AFARI

Yasus Afari (John Sinclair) was born in 1962 in Jamaica and has been performing as a dub poet since the early 1980s. He was then a student at the College of Arts, Science and Technology (today called U-Tech) in Kingston and his performances there were well-received.

Although he had been active as a performer throughout the 1980s, Yasus Afari really came to the Jamaican public's attention in February 1993 when Mutabaruka handed him his JAMI award on stage and asked him to accept it.

1993 saw the release of *Dancehall Baptism*, a brave attempt at fusing dancehall music with the dub poetry art form and a reaction against the slackness which had gripped dancehall in the late 1980s. The CDs *Mental Assassin* and *Honour Crown Him* followed in 1995 and 1997 respectively. *Gif of Vision* was released in 2000, and *Revolution Chapter* One in 2007.

Yasus Afari's first collection of poems, *Eye Pen*, was published in 1998, and contained some of the pieces he had recorded, like "Patwah Talkin" or "Dreadlocks Dinner". The latter track was performed on stage with Black Uhuru in the 1990s and is of course based on the famous Black Uhuru hit "Guess Who's Coming to Dinner, Natty Breadlocks".

Over the years Afari has collaborated with many reggae artists, like Garnett Silk (they recorded a version of Johnny Nash's "I Can See Clearly Now"), Beres Hammond, Luciano, Freddie McGregor and Singing Melody. His work with these recording artistes is a kind of bridge between dancehall and dub poetry, and certainly shows that poetry can be made accessible to a wider public. So Yasus Afari seems to be constantly on the move and pushing barriers.

In 2007 *Overstanding Rastafari: Jamaica's Gift to the World* was published and was greeted by Professor Barry Chevannes of UWI as a "theological tour de force" and an "ecumenical" book on Rastafari (*The Gleaner*, "Yasus to Jamaica", April 14,

2007). It is Yasus's attempt at explaining Rastafari to the rest of the world and certainly an insider's view on the movement.

In 2013 Afari released *Public Secret*, an album which was entirely recorded with his own band, Dub Vijan, and in 2016 *Vocal Ink: The Mental Intercourse* was published. Afari's latest book is a mixture of poetry and prose which was endorsed by the University of the West Indies' Department of Literature.

Interview (Mandeville, 20 August 2008)

Interviewer: You came upon the poetry performance scene in the early 1990s when Mutabaruka handed you his JAMI award. That's when many people, including myself, first became aware of your work. So how long had you been peforming when Mutabaruka handed you his award?

Yasus Afari:Well, it depends on how you check it. Professionally we started performing at the dawn of the 1990s, but we had been performing publicly since the late '80s. I started writing while I was at school in the late '70s, and then I continued writing while I was with the Jamaica Telephone Company here in Mandeville between 1980 and 1982, and I then I got a scholarship to CAST [the College of Arts, Science and Technology, now known as Utech]. We did our first public performance in late 1983 at CAST. I was hosting an event. And then I recorded for GG Records in 1987. So essentially we started working in the late 1980s, professionally in the early 1990s, and came to national attention in the early 1990s, and one of these events was the one you just alluded to which was on February 23rd 1993.

I: In Europe at the time it seemed as if Muta was passing the baton to the next generation of dub poets...

YA: What happened is that Muta called me and handed me the award publicly, and I refused, and I asked the crowd and said: "People, we live in a democratic country, we need a consensus, what should I do?". They said: "Take it!" and they gave a standing ovation, and then I did. But Muta was saying: "What kinda t'ing dat, bredren? How me a give you a award and you no want it and you ask de people?". And I said: "OK, we give thanks". So essentially it was a very poetic moment of justice and judgement, because Muta said he thinks I was more deserving after all the work I'd been doing over the years in question.

I: You're variously known as a poet, performance poet or dub poet. Are you comfortable with all those "labels"?

YA: I am not a person for "labels", and I don't have a real issue with "labels". I'm into charting new courses, establishing new precedents. I'm into creating news areas of avenues and different ways of doing things. So therefore I redefine new definitions constantly. But largely speaking if people define me as a dub poet, based on my understanding of dub poetry, I don't have a problem with that. Neither do I have a problem with being a poet or a performance poet. In these different instances it helps to clarify what you do. So maybe all of these titles are true? No-one in terms of perception, definition and meaning would encapsulate and sum up all that I do.

I: Your first album, entitled *Dancehall Baptism*, was released in 1993 by RAS Records and contained a song in which you said that you wanted to purify or to cleanse the dancehall. Were you referring then to the slackness and gun lyrics that dominated Jamaican music in the late 1980s?

YA: The negativity which was evident in the music, and still is, so this a work in progress actually. I didn't pretend it was a one-off situation. It was important at the moment to have arrested the situation and to have offered some healthy alternative in my opinion. The need still arises today; it is a constant need to have something positive. But nevertheless every moment of our history has been suffused with good and bad. So we have to accentuate the positive and hopefully the positive will overwhelm the negative. What happened in that instance is that the heritage and legacy of people like Bob Marley, and Peter Tosh, and Bunny Wailer, and Jimmy Cliff, and other people who used the music as a medium, as an instrument of liberation and public information, we wanted to preserve that heritage, we wanted to contribute to that heritage, and we see that there were elements and institutions of government at work to derail and subvert and undermine the dignity and integrity of our music and our culture. We wanted to challenge that. So therefore we set out to orchestrate a change whereby we worked on the current dancehall riddims with a positive message; we went to the dancehall space with an uplifting message. We promoted events with an upfull, positive emphasis. When we do interviews, we always try to accentuate the positive, we lifestyle, the things we embrace. Garnett Silk was a product of that excercise, people like Luciano, Sizzla, Buju Banton, Kulcha Knox, Uton Green, Everton Blenda, and there are several others.

I: On your first CD, there were two tracks which were outstanding: "Patwah Talking" and "Teachings of Marcus", which are also in your collection entitled *Eye Pen.* So apparently Marcus Garvey and Louise Bennett are two of your heroes.

YA: Well, you would haffe call Miss Lou a "shero"! We consider Miss Lou as the mother of the Jamaican indigenous tongue and by virtue of that, she is the mother of Jamaica. In that poem we say that "a Miss Lou a di mother fi patwah/And she would haffe tell oonu a who a the father". So quite possibly Marcus Garvey can be considered as a candidate. But these people are people who have contributed a lot to Jamaica, to black people, and to humanity. And we really have to celebrate and value them for that. Marcus Garvey was one of the greatest leaders within the black community and the world community. Miss Lou, by her impact on the Jamaican culture and language, she added an element of dignity to the language, acceptability, and we know that language shapes and conditions the thinking. Therefore somebody who contributes to the development of the language certainly in the same measure contributes to thedevelopment of the mind and the thinking and the mindset of the Jamaican people, and we value Miss Lou for that. I recorded this poem in the early 1990s, and it is being re-released now based on the attention that the Jamaican language is now getting. The Jamaica Language Unit at the University of the West Indies (UWI) will be publishing *The Jamaica Language Dictionary* in November of this year. I was a poet in residence in Birmingham the other day and one of my first assignments was to award a certificate to the students graduating in the Jamaican *language* course that is now recognised by the Institute of Linguistics in the UK. What we call Jamaican patois is now regarded as the Jamaican language, and in education, in the judiciary services, in health services, and specifically mental health, the language is now being revisited and seen as a medium of challenging problems in education, in judiciary services and in mental health. Also there are students being offered the Jamaican language at the A Level in the UK

I: What about the situation in Jamaica? Do you think that there is more acceptance of the Jamaican language than 20 years ago? Has progress been made?

YA: Yes, I think so! Because you hear it in the media, especially television and the radio, and in the press also. Once, you know, you could get fired from a job for speaking in patois. Now you have programmes and newscasts. The *Jamaican Language Dictionary* is now done and will be launched in November. The Parliament actually gave a mandate to the Language Unit to do a project on the Jamaican language. They completed the project last year in August. When the Jamaican language is used in the classroom, it deepens student participation and it deepens democracy, so you can see it everyday, it's a medium of empowering the students.

I: You released other CDs like *Mental Assassin* and *The Gift of*

Vision on which you recorded tracks with reggae singers like Luciano, Garnett Silk, Natural Black, Freddie McGregor and Black Uhuru. So you seem to be pushing boundaries and to be redefining the boundaries between dub poet and entertainer or recording artiste.

YA: I wanted to show at the time that poetry is flexible and applicable to different situations. It can be entertaining and edutaining at the *same* time. I didn't try to demonstrate it by collaborating with these artistes. It just happened by a natural synergy, actually organically. Actually I was in the studio with Garnett Silk in 1990 and he insisted that we do something together. So we did "I Can See Clearly", which was the first combination I did. And then the one with Luciano, I produced it and Luciano suggested we do a combination on that track. Blackbeard, Tappa Zukie's brother, suggested the combinations with Freddie McGregor and Beres Hammond.

I: Your poem entitled "Dreadlocks Dinner", which can be found in your *Eye Pen* collection and on your *Gift of Vision* CD, was obviously inspired by the Black Uhuru classic "Guess Who's Coming to Dinner, Natty Dreadlock". Tell me about this poem.

YA: Hear what happen now! I was on tour with Black Uhuru at the time and the group was headed by Don Carlos. So we had "Mercy Street" and "Brand New World" which we were promoting at the time. So they called me up on stage to do "Mercy Street" and "Brand New World", and Don Carlos just started singing "Guess Who's Coming to Dinner, Natty Dreadlock" almost on the spot! They were feeling so good, my performance was so well received and people came to anticipate my return on stage. So it was a spur-of-the-moment thing and I did some lyrics: "Mi waan vegetable, fruits and marijuana/Roots, nuts and mash pitata".

I: Focusing now on some of your poems in the *Eye Pen* collection, there's a poem entitled "Maurice Bishop". When did you write this poem?

YA: In 1983! It was during the time I was at college and a lot of Grenadians were with us at college also. We were very in tune to the regional politics and geopolitics, and to the socio-economic realities of the world, and somehow it inspired me to register my comments on the issue. I peformed it on campus and it was very popular.

I: Another of your poem is "Battle of Adowa". It sounds like a chant. Have you ever recorded that one?

YA: Never! What happened is that I visited Ethiopia at the invitation of the Ethiopian government in 1996 to commemorate the centenary of the battle of Adowa. The battle of Adowa, for those who might not know, really came about when Italy invaded Ethiopia in 1896, when Menelik II was Emperor of Ethiopia. The Italians wanted to lord it over Ethiopia as the Protectorate of Ethiopia, and Menelik would have none of it. So war was as a result of Ethiopia trying to defend her age-old sovereignty and territorial integrity, and independence. So they went to war and they defeated what was perceived to be an invincible European force, with comparatively primitive weapons. But with a just cause, and faith, Menelik II proved that even in that time, David could defeat Goliath, as His Imperial Majesty did in the 1930s, when Italy again invaded Ethiopia. So we were there in 1996 to commemorate the centenary and that inspired "The Battle of Adowa" and several other poems like "In the Emperor's Bed". We ended up sleeping in the Emperor's bed when we were in Ethiopia! "Mama Lake Tana" was also written while my feet were dabbling in the Lake Tana.

I: In March 2007, you published a new book on Rastafari. Many books have been written about Rastafari. What can we expect from that one? What makes it so special?

YA: Well, hear this now! The more things change, the more they remain the same, and the more they remain the same, the more they change. There's nothing new under the sun, but we need to be reminded, we need a new perpspective, a new vantage point. We need to add more *voices* to the chorus. This book, *Overstanding Rastafari*, is written by a member of the Rastafari family, which makes it more real than other things which have been written. Now, there is a lack of material about Rastafari and I was asked by the Ministry of Education to address that as a cultural agent. So we are intimate with the questions that are being asked by the educators and the students in the school system. And I travel the world, and people always come and ask me about Rastafari, about how we can use the Rastafari worldview to lend ideas and inspiration to different other issues and struggles all over the world. So we tabulated all of these questions and subjects brought into the curriculum and people's questions and addressed these issues comprehensively. The book consists of 21 chapters with a lot of context. So this book is different and unique against that background of being devoted to the faith in excess of 25 years, and out of that experience, this is a response to provide information which was hitherto *lacking* , largely speaking. So the success of the book is testament to its relevance: we sold the first print in less than a month.

MOQAPI SELASSIE

Moqapi Selassie is a performance poet of Jamaican parentage who was born in England and who has been writing and performing in the UK for many years now. He was born and raised in Birmingham and thus belongs to the Black British generation, the children of Jamaican immigrants who settled down in the UK in the late 1940s and throughout the 1950s.

In his teens Moqapi became attracted to the reggae and Rastafarian subculture which had taken Britain by storm in the 1970s following the success of bands like Bob Marley and the Wailers, Third World, Culture and the Gladiators. In the early 1980s Black Uhuru came on the scene and made a very big impression with songs like "Abortion", "Plastic Smile" and "Guess Who's Coming to Dinner". They quickly became Moqapi's favourite band.

Moqapi also became a member of the Ethiopian World Federation, a Rastafarian organisation which had been responsible for the repatriation of Rastafarians to Ethiopia (Shashamene). He also joined a sound system called Wassifa International and learnt how to play the akete drum.

Over the years Moqapi has established quite a reputation as a dub poet or a performance poet.

Interview (Birmingham, 16 August 1999):

Interviewer: Moqapi, you were born in England, of Jamaican parentage. So the first thing I would ask you would be how it felt to grow up in England as a black British person, and how much has this influenced your work. Do you consider yourself as a "black British person"? Do you like that phrase?

Moqapi Selassie: I don't know when you say "British", to me, it always reminds me of the White Anglo-Saxon Protestants, so I'd define myself as an African, an Ethiopian. Other people will say "Well, you were born in Britain, you've got black skin, so, therefore you're black British", but I see myself as an Ethiopian here in England. So that's how I see myself.

I Did you have to put up with a lot of racism?

MS: Oh yeah, definitely. I mean, that's what you grew up with. You grew up with it from school days, in the playground. Before you got to the playground, just walking down the street and it was "blackie, blackie, wog, nigger, coon". So you grew up with it and when you went to school, it was the same thing. So from you're about five years old, you had to deal with it, and of course, at that time, when someone called you "blackie", it was like a negative term. So when someone called you "blackie", you jumped up and thumped him. So you grew up fighting in England, you know what I mean. Being black, you learnt to fight, 'cause that's what you had to do most of the time.

I: Do you feel that the situation today, now that you're an adult, is slightly better than when you were a kid? Have things improved for the black community in England or is the situation the same as when you were a kid?

MS: I think it's like a relative improvement in the sense that, I don't think you see that much now, like when we were coming up, it was so open, but now I think it's more subtle. Before you had all kinds of racism, you had the institutionalised, you had the overt. I think, like the overt racism now, you don't find it that much. I don't know if it's because of the legislation and all them kind of things, the laws they have been putting against it, so if you called someone a nigger, you could be taken to court, but the institutionalised racism, that still exists.

I: So, now, moving on to your poetry and your writing, when did you first get interested in poetry?

MS: First that would mean school. We did poetry in school, in junior school, about six or seven, and I also used to go to the library. We started doing poetry in school and the teacher would say "Have a go at writing poetry!" and then when I wrote the poem, the teacher would say "yeah, that's all right". So it started from there. Then I went to a secondary modern school and we did poetry there as well and I wrote some poems for the school magazine. Then, in my teens I think it was, I wanted to be a writer, so I would kind of work on my poetry. But writing in patois now, that started like, going back to when I used to go to the library and get books from Louise Bennett. So I got poetry books out and read different kinds of poetry, but Louise Bennett's poetry now, that kind of poetry hit me because when I read it, I could relate it to my parents, my brothers, my sisters and so forth, and I never actually tried writing like that until the dub poets came and started to deal with dub poetry and that's when I started writing like in patois or creole.

I: So, you've just mentioned Louise Bennett and the dub poets. Do you consider yourself as a dub poet, a performance poet, a black poet, or just a poet?

MS: A dub poet. That's how I see myself.

I: So, what's the difference between a dub poet and a performance poet? Why do you insist on the term "dub"?

MS: Because I think that term came out to describe that genre of poetry, dub poetry I think that dub poetry lends itself to performance. Performance poetry could be like any kind of poetry in the sense that it could be performed in English, in standard English, or in a dialect of English and that would be performance poetry, whereas dub poetry, I see it as a different genre that fits into that classification.

I: Has it got to be in dialect to be dub poetry or could you write a dub poem in standard English?

MS: It doesn't necessarily have to be in patois for it to be a dub poem.

I: To some poets, the term "dub poetry" is limited. There was a big controversy over ten years ago when Jean Binta Breeze said she found dub too limited because she felt she had to write about certain things in a certain mode, and she wanted to move out of it. So when you write, do you make a conscious decision to write in patois or in standard English or does it come just like that? Do you do it on the spur of the moment or do you think "I'm gonna write this poem in standard English; I'm gonna write that one in patois"?

MS: Poems come differently...I suppose it's just the vibes of the times but saying it's just the vibes of the times is just a cop-out really. You work at it, you know what I mean To me patois lends itself to dub poetry, so that's the form I would use. I feel that when you're talking about Jean Binta Breeze and the ones who say it's limited, I see that as a load of bullshit! Because dub poetry is there You don't have to limit yourself. If you're a poet per se, you don't have to limit yourself at all. If you can write in iambic pentametre, perfect standard English and if that's the vibe that poem comes in, then you write it like that. I could write a poem in Birmingham slang if I thought that it needed to be put across that way. So I don't see it as being limited. It's up to the poems.

I: Moving on to one of your poems more specifically. The last time I met you, you mentioned a poem entitled "Confidence". Is it about confidence as a black person in Britain, or a more general poem?

MS: I think "Confidence" as a poem applies to anyone really [then launches into "Confidence"]. So I think that's just universal.

I: Yes, definitely! I like the interplay between the musical parts and the rest of the poem. Was that poem influenced by DJ music, because I hear some DJ influence in the musical chant.

MS: Definitely, 'cause way back in my teens, that's what I used to do, I used to deejay...

I: It's funny how many dub poets started out...

MS: as DJs, yeah! [bursts out laughing]

I: Levi Tafari told me that he started out as a DJ performing on a sound system as well, and Adisa too...So it seems like a natural move to make. So do you perform "Confidence" regularly?

MS: Oh, yeah! I've done "Confidence" in schools, I've done "Confidence" in prisons, I've done "Confidence" in churches. I always do "Confidence" because I feel it's universal. "Confidence" isn't talking about like racism or being a dreadlocks. To do anything, you need confidence.

I: When we last met in 1998 you mentioned a poem entitled

"Bad Boy in America", so I was wondering whether it was about crime in New York or in Miami...

MS: No, no, no It's about America! I think I just looked at the situation now in the world, and it's like if something happens in Africa, like Somalia, or for example Lybia, America is like the world's police. America portrays itself as a bad boy, like when they talk about yardies and so forth, that's how America portrays itself; as a bad boy. If you joke with America, if you mess with America, anyone, they'll go over there and they'll bump you off! It's like Grenada, they went over there So that's what it's saying "Bad Boy in America" is talking about that American attitude that says "If you mess with me, I'll kick your ass".

I: That one would be going down very well in France! The last time I met you, you also mentioned a very controversial poem that raised a few eyebrows when you performed it. That was "Batty Bwoy Bizniz". So is it something like Buju Banton's "Boom Bye Bye"? Is it a homophobic piece?

MS: No! It's not saying "go out and kill homosexuals". I think that was what "Boom Bye Bye" was saying, but all I'm saying is "well, to me, it's not right". That's all "Batty Bwoy Bizniz" is saying, really. [then performs the poem].

I: You told me you had some hostile reactions when you performed it.

MS: What happened was that...I was at the Round Festival in Dorset. It's a place called Wimborne and they perform in the round. They perform poetry or plays in the round and, as opposed to the proscenium arch where you've got the audience in front of you, they look at it as a kind of revolutionary statement, cause if you go uptown and start talking poetry, people will gather around you, whereas with the proscenium arch, you're in control, because no one is behind you. Anyway, I did a performance and then I came off, and they said "Well, do something else", and I did "Batty Bwoy Bizniz". Then one person jumped up and crossed, and kissed his lover, and that was it basically. I mean, it wasn't as if they were gonna lynch me. And a woman did say to me "Why did you do that poem? You spoilt the whole evening", and then the next day, she said "I think you were right to do the poem", so that was it really.

I: What kind of poetry do you read? What is your main source of inspiration?

MS: I read dub poetry I check for Louise Bennett, because she's like the godmother..., you know what I mean, I wouldn't do dub poetry if there wasn't Louise Bennett! I like all the dub poets: Mikey Smith, Mutabaruka, Linton Kwesi Johnson over here, Zephaniah. And even the DJs too, you know what I mean...

I: Do you have any favourite DJs currently?

MS: Nowadays, I like DJs like Sizzla, Anthony B, Determine, them kind of DJs.

I By the way, someone recently told me that Determine was popular as a poet too! Are you aware of that?

MS: No, I didn't know I reckon most of them must have touched poetry. I think it's like a very close thing between dub poetry and deejaying. You could say that dub poets are frustrated DJs or the other way round! As you said, most of the dub poets started out on a sound system.

I: Zephaniah used to deejay on sounds, Levi Tafari, Adisa One final question maybe. Is Moqapi Selassie a happy man?

MS: Yes! I mean like poetically-wise, yes. To me, I just know that there's a lot of work to do. I mean there's poems to get published, there's CDs to get done, so yeah I've got a CD at the moment. How shall I put it It's not finalised yet, but I've gone to the studio, I've done everything. Basically, all I need to do is to go there and pick it up and take it from there. But they were just a cappella pieces. I've got a CD-rom project, it's taking ages for it to be authored, but we've done the video part of it, so it's just for the persons to finish it up. So, I mean, poetically-wise, it's only a few people that make money out of poetry and the only way you do that is by getting stuff out there. So I'm in a poetry group called the Conscious Poets' Society and things are all right. It's better than it was and it's not as good as it's gonna be!

Interview update (June 2017):

I: In 2010 you wrote a play entitled *Blackheart Man* which you took to the stage and performed at various venues in the West Midlands. Can you tell me more about this play?

MS: Yeah, *Blackheart Man* came about like this. James Pogson, who ended up directing the piece, used to see me performing poetry and after a number of performances he would ask me if I'd ever thought of doing a one-man show. In fact, he would state "you need to do a one-man show". At the time I never thought about it too much; however, an opportunity came up at The Drum for local artists to develop their ideas and bring them to performance. I wanted to tell the story of the first generation of Black people born here in the UK, what it was like growing up in a Jamaican family in England and what becoming a Rastafarian meant. The things ones had to go through. That's how *Blackheart Man* came about.
Now growing up in England as children there was always the tale of the 'Bogey Man' – a mythical character used to control the behaviour of children. When we were young we were told not to stay out too late or the 'Bogey Man' would get you. Well, in Jamaica there is the 'Blackheart Man' who was the original Rastaman. And just like the 'Bogey Man' in the UK the Blackheart Man was used to strike fear into the minds of children. However, unlike the Bogey Man the Rastafarian actually existed and in Jamaica he was reviled and abused., rejected and scorned. Bunny Wailer has a classic album called *Blackheart Man* which details this. I took the concept of the Blackheart Man and placed him in the UK because becoming

a Rastafari in those times was a struggle, it meant immediate rejection by family and friends, so that's why I used that title. The character Leroy Jones is the Blackheart Man. The show incorporates monologues, poetry, song and music. It's like a trip down memory lane.

I: A few years ago, you were involved in a project called *The Word Temple*. What did it consist of?

MS: The *Word Temple* was the brainchild of Amani Naphthali, who as far as I am concerned is one of the UK's most underated playwrights/ directors/ producers/ theatre practitioners. He wrote and directed such plays as *Song of Songs*, and *Ragamuffin* and directed *Modern Amazons* amongst many others. Anyway, he had the idea of taking the spoken word and delivering it in a theatrical context, he based this concept around the Last Poets notion of poetry being "spographics" that is, spoken graphics. He worked with the poets not just delivering the poems but performing them like a theatrical piece. That was one aspect of *The Word Temple* but he also incorporated a DJ, a live band and singers. and video footage. I performed in two out of three manifestations of the *Word Temple*. We toured it in 2005 and 2006. In 2005 there was I, Moqapi Selassie, David J, the lyrical pugilist, Kim Trusty, Michelle Scally Clarke, Ekundayo, Gemma Weekes, Stella (the Musical Director) and a host of others I can't remember right now. The *Word Temple* was truly groundbreaking, it has been copied many times, but nothing I've seen has ever come near to it.

I: What is the state of dub poetry today in England and in Jamaica? Is it still a relevant art form?

MS: Good question. I would say that from a certain perspective dub poetry in the UK has been confined to the annals of history, something of the 1980s when Linton Kwesi Johnson and Benjamin Zephaniah were in their prime. What do I mean by that? Although there are dub poets here in the UK the main focus has been on Linton Kwesi Johnson and Benjamin Zephaniah. On the female side we had Jean Binta Breeze who has returned to Jamaica, I think. Both LKJ and Jean Binta Breeze fought against being defined as "dub poets". Zephaniah said he was a "dub ranter". Which to I is really strange: dub poets not wanting to be called dub poets. How can a genre survive if its leading practitioners don't want to be known by the genre they are promoting. It's like Bob Marley saying he is just a musician and that he just plays music, not Roots Rock Reggae. Come on. So yes, I'n'I see that there are no youth dub poets that are coming up. I would go as far as saying it was dub poetry that inspired and initiated the whole spoken word phenomenon in the UK. Well, that's how dub poetry is defined in the UK. So I don't see any of the youths…

I: How has the recent closing down of The Drum affected performance poetry in Birmingham?

MS: It has affected it in that it was the premier black arts venue in the UK and Birmingham's black community's main venue and there were many poetry events that were staged there. From the very first Poetry Cafe events that was hosted by the Conscious Poets Society, of which I was a member, to Griotology that was hosted by Kokumo and other poetry events. So in many respects the Drum's closing down has not only affected performance poetry, but the whole of black arts in the Midlands and the UK.

I: Where do you perform these days?

MS: I do the occasional performance here and there, community centres, parties, shows, festivals and, of late, funerals. Yeah I know! It's a strange one, but I've been requested to do them, and as a community artist, I've done them. More time I'm working on my long-awaited album. So that's what I'm focusing on at the moment.

KOKUMO NOXID

Gerald Dixon, aka Kokumo, was born in Jamaica. He is a Rastafarian. He has lived in Birmingham for many years and is well-known as a dub poet, workshop facilitator and storyteller. For a few years he ran a 'griottology' workshop at the Drum, in Aston, where he compered several events like the tribute to Louise Bennett in September 2006.

Kokumo visits Jamaica regularly and has worked with the noted dub poet Yasus Afari, releasing a CD single with him entitled "Set it Off". In 2006 Kokumo released a CD entitled *Writing's on the Wall*, recorded in Birmingham with local musicians. His first collection of poems, *Dub Truth*, was published in 2016 and the follow up *Pipe Dream* in 2018.

Interview (1 February 2007 and 31 August 2007, Central Library, Birmingham):

Interviewer: Kokumo, you're originally from Jamaica.

Kokumo: I am, I am. Came here a few years ago, nine years ago, checked the scene and met with guys like Moqapi [Selassie], Martin Glynn, and we just started from there. So there was already a scene that existed.

I: Was it easy to fit into that scene?

K: It was, it was, because I was doing, I am doing dub poetry, so it was, in a sense, organic.

I: So you would define yourself as a dub poet mainly?

K: Yes, a dub poet, and at one stage, I was doing more gigs, I was singing more than I was doing poetry. But I realised that dub poetry gives a more direct message in a sense. People take you more seriously when you're doing dub poetry, you have something to say. So when you strip it down and take away some of the elements, people tend to pay attention.

I: And when you were in Jamaica, who were your main mentors or inspirations? People like Mutabaruka?

K: There were loads, there were loads. And even before I discovered Muta, I discovered Oku.

I: Okuonuora (Orlando Wong)?

K: Yes, as a real revolutionary when it comes to dub poetry. And of course the late great Michael Smith. So there was always the influence… It was a combination of the dub poetry and the reggae music.

I: Out of Oku, Muta and Mikey, which one would you say influenced you the most in your approach to poetry?

K: I think Muta, to be honest with you, I think Muta, because you were hearing more of Muta's stuff on the radio. In a sense I'm not gonna label Muta as commercial but in that sense we were hearing more of Muta's stuff. To hear Oku and Mikey Smith you would have had to pick up books, but you could switch on the radio and you could hear Muta. And of course, you know, Muta had a radio programme called "Cutting Edge", and you could hear his poetry.

I: I heard that "Cutting Edge" in Jamaica has become something of an institution, it's become very popular…

K: It is, it is. It's more like an intellectual institution in the sense that it educates and it creates an awareness. There will always be that element in Jamaica, but from that level which is Afrocentric, it is, you know, "cutting edge".

I: I suppose there was a big controversy when it first came on the air…

K: Yes, there was because in a society where elitism exists to one extreme, you know, anything that challenges that, there's gonna be a problem. There were controversies, but it's still carrying on, you know…

I: It's a phone-in show: you can phone and give your opinion.

K: Yes, it's interactive. It's that kind of openenness.

I: You've mentioned informal influences like Muta, "Cutting

Edge", but did you study at the University of the West Indies?

K: No, I didn't reach...Well I reached Extra-Mural, which is an extension of the University, but I never studied at University. Then I kind of get caught up with some of Marcus Garvey's teachings. My elder brother used to have books on Marcus Garvey. When you discover this literature, then you get into that mood. I think to me it took a journey and a journey of kind of re-discovery of I-self in the sense that some of the awareness opened up even more so when I came to this country because when you start to see things from a different spectrum, then it makes it more interesting.

I: Was there a particular reggae artist who had a very big influence on you as a poet?

K: Yes, I think the music of Peter Tosh because being a revolutionary, I saw music as speaking directly to people to open up people's consciousness, you understand. So to me I just like Peter, who was very outspoken.

I: Talking about your growing-up process in Jamaica, when you were at school, in primary school, or secondary school, what kind of poetry did you study?

K: Louise Bennett! I mean I didn't have to study it: it was just there, you understand! You just recited Louise Bennett's poetry. There was a programme on TV, every Saturday. Louise Bennett was always a part of that process, you know. Later on, I came across Langston Hughes... I didn't come across Langston Hughes until very late.

I: So you were aware of a poetic tradition...

K: Yes, yes. And the storytelling tradition was always there, so it wasn't too far from the poetry .

I: What about Ranny Williams?

K: Ranny Williams? That was mainly stage. They used to do radio plays and pantomime. So he was very big on the pantomime scene. They used to work together.

I: Why did you come to England?

K: It was mainly to further my education, because education is a journey and I don't see education as purely academic. And also for employment because we always lived with the notion that the streets of England are paved with gold!

I: Well, was it what you expected?

K: No, I never had that expectation! You come and see for yourself, you know, and reality hits you. There's no such thing!

I: Are there more opportunities for you as a performance poet over here than in Jamaica?

K: Yes, and no! Why I say no, is that I went to Jamaica and what I discovered there is that if I was in Jamaica I would be probably I-ver more popular as a dub poet than I am here and I think it's because of the direct connection with America and elsewhere. The thing with here is, if you're gonna look at how events are programmed here, they are very much based on funding and stuff like that and it might seem as if there are more opportunities, but in Jamaica on the other hand there's always the aspect of creating these opportunities. There is now an international festival called "Calabash" in May and that opened up different perspectives.

I: Talking about your work now more specifically. Last September, on September 29th, there was an event at The Drum as a tribute to Louise Bennett that you hosted or compered…

K: Yes, in fact, I coordinated the whole tribute…I was Resident Poet at The Drum for two and a half years, so when Miss Lou passed on, they approached me and said, you know, would I like to do something. You know, I think I would have felt guilty if I hadn't done anything. So it was like a call of duty to do it.

I: On that day, you were introducing the main performers and between the performances, you did something which to me is very reminiscent of what Mutabaruka does. Muta is famous for his ability to relate to the audience and for his between-poems patter…

K: It's part of the tradition, the oral tradition, the storytelling tradition, yes, it calls for interaction. As a performer, that's what you have to be able to do, because if you're not reaching the audience, then basically what you're doing is…So you've got to be able to reach the audience. So there's a little bit of humour, and then there's the seriousness, because if you give the dose too strong, they're not gonna be able to take it. It's gotta be little.

I: A lot of your poems are protest poems. Do you consider yourself as a political poet?

K: I think I'm more of a cultural activist and my poetry looks at political issues that affect people's lives.

I: How would define your role as a dub poet or as a poet?

K: I think my role as a dub poet/poet is to continue to raise awareness, and heighten people's consciousness through word sound and power.

I:Do you write more about Jamaica or about England?

K: I think it's global. There are five or six pieces that I wrote that are definitely about Jamaica. One of the first pieces I wrote about Jamaica was a poem called "Nuh Weh Nuh Betta dan Yard". And that was about the whole conception of what England was supposed to be, and when I came to see how it is, you think "no way no better than yard"!

I: Was Admiral Bailey's song of the same name an inspiration?

K: That was also an inspiration, but it was an experience as well, as to what I saw.

I: This poem is obviously about the disappointment felt by many Jamaican people when they first came to England? Don't you think that the situation has somewhat improved for the Jamaican/West Indian community in England, at least economically? Or is it as bad as in the 1950s or 1970s?

K: I personally don't think things have gotten better for us; I think we've just found a better way of coping with the conditions.

I: The poem entitled "A One Jamaikan Dis" is a very strong piece about tackling the negative stereotypes Jamaicans are burdened with (violence, drugs). How did you come to write this poem? Was it out of personal experience?

K: Yes, it was part personal and the rest is down to my observations of how we are portrayed in the media as Jamaicans.

I: "Another One OD'ed Again" is about the drugs problem in the black community. Or could it be about other communities? What moved you to write this poem?

K: This is a general problem that affects all communities not just blacks - however this piece focuses on the black communities.

I: "Mista Government Man" is a strong protest piece. What's or who's the main target in this piece?

K: This piece is directed to any system that is set up to exploit and oppress people in general, and yes it's my personal views on government systems.

I: What about the name "Kokumo"?

K: It's Yoruba and it means "this one will not die". The whole thing about that is that after I and I pass on to the ancestors, you live on and the name "Kokumo" does not mean that Kokumo will not die, but that the work of Kokumo will live on forever.

I: There are various Rastafarian sects: the Twelve Tribes of

Israel, the Ethiopian World Federation, the Bobo Dreads...

K: I'm part of the Bobo Ashanti. Well, as you can see , the visual representation of wearing a turban, that is one of the main connotations. So you can easily identify a Bobo Ashanti by his turban and so on...

I: And his staff as well?

K: And his staff as well! It is a very important part of the grounding as well.

I: Is it the most popular branch of Ratsafarianism in Jamaica now?

K: I think it is *now*, I think it is. It wasn't certainly in the 1980s and the 1990s coming up, it wasn't, but I think there has been a kind of surge of the movement; I think it's probably because of the popularity of people like Sizzla, Capleton, Anthony B. who've embraced that particular sect. So it has created a kind of surge within the young Rastafarians to become a part of what is seen as *militant*, even though I don't think Bobo Ashanti was seen as the most militant of all. The Nyabinghis were more of a militant sect, but I think now the Bobo Ashanti feel that.

I: Are the Bobo Ashanti accepted by the authorities in Jamaica?

K: I think they are tolerated; accepted? No. There is still this continuous struggle with authority and one of the main problems for that is the use of the holy sacrament, which is the herb or marijuana. That still is a big problem, a major problem. The problem is accepting the system, the Babylonian system. The ways of the Jamaican élite are still there. So therefore accepting Rastafari, I don't think Jamaica is ready for that.

I: If you had to sum up in a few words the differences between a Twelve Tribes dread and a Bobo Dread, what would these differences be?

K: Well, first we drop the dread thing! But I think that, apart from the visual representation, I think that the Twelve Tribes, they are a bit more subtle and a bit more tolerant to certain behaviour or certain systems. I think, to me, they're easier to assimilate or to allow assimilation. With the Bobo Ashanti, we see ourselves as trying to portray this visual image of the positiveness of Rastafari, and I think that's what we do. Yes, the militancy is there through the music, through the spoken word.

I: In terms of doctrine, is there a big difference between Bobo Ashantis and Twelve Tribes? Do you all believe in the same god?

K: Yes, the basic principles are the same. It is more a matter of representation. The Twelve Tribes were basically formed by what we call middle-class Jamaican youths, privileged, so they were not from the ghetto, so it was a difference. But the important thing that happened was that they allowed some level of acceptance in Jamaican society, because most of those guys were privileged to go to university and, even though their parents weren't happy with their coming on with dreads and stuff like that, they were happy with them having a degree, so that was acceptable. So they made their way into professional positions. They created a kind of middle ground.

I: Is there a particular place or parish in Jamaica where the Bobo Dreads are more numerous?

K: Well, now it's Bull Bay, but it kind of spread out now, in August Town where Sizzla is from and all those areas.

I: Is it harder to maintain your Rastafarian way of life now that you're in the UK?

K: Well, the movement has been tarnished with negative stereotypes, we know that, but I think in today's modern society, there is a level of acceptance. So on the surface I don't see a problem, but underneath or behind it might mean that people will have second thoughts, but personally I don't think it has affected me in any way.

I: Your poem entitled "A One Jamaikan Dis" obviously tackles the issue of racial stereotyping.

K: What happened was that, you know, I was on the radio, and there was a presenter, and she was supposed to be doing Caribbean news, and unfortunately it was mainly news coming from Jamaica, and in some way, she was kind of reinforcing all the negative stereotypes. So I ended up writing a letter to the chairman, saying I'm disgusted with this. Most of the portrayal on television of what's coming out of Jamaica is negative. I remember there was a film, called *The Yardies* or whatever, that came out on Channel Four, and it was fuelling all those stereotypes. So that's how that piece came about.

I: You also wrote a nostalgic piece about Jamaica called "Nu Weh Nu Betta Dan Yard". Tell me about that phrase, because I've heard it in many songs.

K: Yes, it's been used in so many songs, because there was a song by Ras Karbi using that phrase. It was part of the Popular Song Contest.

I: You're not only a poet, but also a recording artiste. You released a CD entitled *Writing's On The Wall*. Tell me about the recording process.

K: It was recorded here, at Earth Studio, in Birmingham, and the guys on the CD were guys I went to college with and we've been kind of jamming and gigging for quite some time, and one of the musicians said that I should record an album. So I took the initiative and went into the studio.

I: The title track, "Writing's on the Wall", is obviously a heart-felt piece and a beautiful folk song.

K: If there's a topical issue in the news, then I feel there's a need to reflect that, and "Writing's on the Wall" very much reflects that. There was a famine in Malawi at the time, and the Sudan issue came afterwards.

I: The first track on the CD, "Wounded Soldiers", is a powerful piece of political commentary.

K: It's a reflection on the whole war situation in Iraq, because it was a question of what are we fighting for, how are we gonna benefit as individuals, as persons.

I: You've also recorded a CD single with Yasus Afari, the famous Jamaican dub poet. How did you hook up with Yasus Afari?

K: Well, I wanted to go back to Jamaica to find out about the dub poetry scene, and he became one of my first points of contact. So we did a couple of workshops in schools, and then I ended up peforming at "Poetry in Motion", that's his annual poetry event in Mandeville. So when I went back to Jamaica for the Calabash festival, he said that I had to record something before going back to England.

I: The track is entitled "Set it Off". Why such a title?

K: It's a slang. It means that we want to create an explosion, and if you look at the cover, you see a fire and some flames, so it was that kind of thing.

I: On the track you also use the phrase "bus' out", which reminded me of one of Okuonuora's poems.

K: Yes, he's got a piece called "Bus' Out" and I actually love that piece because in one of my poems I wrote "I want to bus' out like Okuonuora".

I: Is dub poetry "exploding" in Jamaica now?

K: It is! And that track is fitting, you know, because the Amercan TV channel BET, they have done some work in Jamaica with the dub poetry scene, people like Yasus, and some of the younger guys coming through, and they're estimating some 2 million viewers, so it's huge! So all I can say is that dub poetry is certainly "bussing out " in Jamaica right now!

Interview update (May 2017):

I: What is the state of dub poetry today in England and in Jamaica? Is it still a relevant art form?

K: Dub poetry in the UK in my opinion is not taken seriously, because some of the main protagonists, or at least some of those who consider themselves dub poets, lack the true essence of what the genre really means. Dub poetry will remain relevant if the practitioners maintain it in its truest form.

I: When you say that dub poetry is not taken seriously, what do you mean? Is it taken more seriously in Jamaica?

K: Dub poetry as a genre represents the voice of the people. It has always been a direct response to cultural and social norms. With the rise of the far-right in Europe, I don't see any direct responses to those issues coming from those considered as dub poets, either in the UK, or in Jamaica. Jamaica as cultural hub has failed to invest in dub poetry. What I've seen is dub poets having to divert because of the lack of financial gains. However there are dub poets who are trying to keep it alive, people like Ras Takura, Sage, Meeka Natoya, Maverick and Charlie Bobus.

I: What do you mean by "the true essence of what the genre really means "?

K: The true essence of dub poetry is to inform and to invoke conscious responses to cultural and social norms. It must be the voice of the downtrodden.

DREADLOCKALIEN

Richard Grant, aka Dreadlockalien, is well-known as a performance poet, workshop facilitator and slam champion. A chef by trade, he started writing poetry after reading Benjamin Zephaniah's *City Psalms* while at university. In 2003 he won the National Slam Championship in Oxford, and in 2005-2006 he was Birmingham Poet Laureate. He founded the New October Poets collective with Kokumo and Moqapi Selassie, later the Colour Free Visions Team, an organisation which takes poetry to schools and uses oral poetry like slam and grime to reduce illiteracy rates.

Interview (26th February 2008, Birmingham Central Library)

Interviewer: You've made quite a name for yourself over the years as a workshop facilitator, slam champion (in 2003), Birmingham Poet Laureate (in 2005-2006), and now you've got a new project, taking poetry to schools with your Colour Free Visions Team. So how did you get into peformance poetry?

Dreadlockalien: I only came to writing as a career about five or six years ago; originally, I was a chef by trade. So when I left school, I went to art college. Got myself a family very early on, twenty years of age, had children to feed. At the age of twenty-seven, I decided to go back to university. I went to the University of Warwick and I did a degree in social studies, which is a BA, and from there I left the University with a big student's debt. Then I was spotted by an Arts Council officer just before I left who said to me: "That's poetry, what you do". I said: "Oh, really?". All I was doing was reciting a few dub lyrics at a poetry event at the University. I recited a poem that I had written just a year before when I had to do a literature module. We were doing Thomas Hardy, and this wasn't touching my button. Then a teacher gave me *City Psalms*, by Benjamin Zephaniah, and it was the first time I'd read patois, and this was something I could relate to. So I read that book and then went into Linton Kwesi Johnson. And then the jigsaw started to fit into place, tunes I had heard when I was younger, like Linton Kwesi Johnson's "Sonny's Lettah", which I had heard when I was growing up. Then I dabbled with poetry for a while, then became a chef again, to pay the bills, part-time, at the same time trying out my new-found hobby, so to speak. Then coming out of University, I had to make some money, so I brought to poetry the same work ehtic as being a chef; so all these projects reflect the work that I've put into poetry.

I: You mentioned Linton Kwesi Johnson. Was he a main source of inspiration for your work? Are you comfortable wit the label "dub poet"?

DA: I think I have moved away a little bit from 1970s dub poetry, but I'm still very much into oral literature, spoken-word type of poetry. I'm not into the written form at all. However, dub poetry is like the voice of Linton Kwesi Johnson, Moqapi Selassie, and I 've realised I'm from a different generation. I've never been to Jamaica, and a lot of my pieces are about the fact that I'm half-English and half-Jamaican, and I juxtapose the two languages. Also, hip hop came after dub poetry. There was also a guy called Smiley Culture who had a record with lyrics that went "Police officer, don't give me no producer!", which was about as musical as dub poetry was gonna get. And then hip hop came on. My style has been described as "dub and hip hop".

I: You're involved in taking poetry to pupils in schools. So do you see yourself as an educator, some kind of teacher?

DA: I think I use poetry as a vessel. Hip-hop poetry is a vessel for reaching young people. The message or the mission that I'm on is to get young people to look closely at words. Adults, it's too late, words are entrenched, meanings, but young people You know, John Agard came along with the term "half-caste", and a lot of people looked to that word. So that's my kind of mission. I've got some words that I'd like to look at long-term, not necessarily change them in my lifetime, but culturally open a debate on words, *important* words.

I: So when you work with pupils in a school, in practical terms, what do you do exactly?

DA: Well, first of all, I was a black artist, I was a cultural artist in school. October busy, September busy, anything to do with slavery. What I did was I used a huge collection of dolls and sculptures that represent ethnicities, and I used to take that into schools and get pupils to write poems about culture, things like that. However, that was replaced by that huge literacy-based project, so now I'm employed as a writer, not a cultural writer, but a writer, to raise literacy rates with boys. We use slamming, get them into teams, with headset mikes, puffer jackets, very urban, beat-box, to get them to do poems about things that they know, so fashion, football. So what we do is a one-day engagement, short-term empowerment workshop to get mass perception of poetry. What happens is that the lads who do lyrics in grime and hip hop usually don't write anything, and then all of a sudden they write pages and pages. So that's what I do it for!

I: Tell me about the Colour Free Visions Team. Are they people you met working in schools, or that you knew before?

DA: The Colour Free Visions Team are a branch or an extension of a collective that I ran a few years ago called the New October Poets. What happened is that I'd met Moqapi [Selassie] and Kokumo three years running at Black History events. I would travel to Birmingham from Rugby, which is 40 miles away, just to go to these events and see cultural poetry, drumming, and whatever. Then I got in touch with them and I got a few emails from Moqapi and Kokumo, and I said: "Look, why don't we get together outside October?". So we had this idea of being called the New October Poets, and for three years, as a collective, we grew. And we did quite a few significant things. We went to the Tate Britain gallery when they did that first Black History Month event. We went to Ledbury, which is a poetry festival (we quadrupled the ethnic population down there!). The reason the name changed (from New October Poets to Colour Free Visions) is that, after about two years, we were seen as a black poetry collective, and I thought to myself, "no I didn't want to become that, it's a poetry collective". So the name "Colour Free Visions" was naturally born, and it says 'We're not a black poetry collective". It came out of the New October Poets, which was poetry of black origin.

I: You're known as a performance poet mainly and as slam champion. So basically how do you memorise all those words? Do you have a particular technique?

DA: I've got an MP3 recorder, so I record the first cut. Usually I've got a scribble, not in full writing, then a CD, and I burn it in the car. And I don't have a phone, so my journey in my car is my peace time, and I can play a poem twenty times. So subconsciously that goes in.

I: Maybe one final question. What about your pen name? Where does that come from?

DA: There three main reasons really. One is that my real name is Richard Grant, and there's already a famous actor in this country called Richard E. Grant. At two or three poetry events they put my name on, and people came expecting someone else So I needed a pseudonym or something like that.

Also at university I was working with a chap who was doing lexicography, the study of words, and I was looking for two of the most marketable words in the next 50 years for youth culture. We put loads of words like "urban", and so on and so forth, but "dreadlock" and "alien" came up. When I was younger, I was always the one asking questions about conspiracy theories and aliens.

The third reason basically is because I do feel alienated from all different cultures.

MBALA

Mbala is usually considered a dub poet by academics and in the *Oxford Book of Caribbean Poetry,* Stewart Brown and Mark Mc Watt defined him as a "dub or a performance poet" (Brown and Mc Watt 368). He was involved in the Spanish Town-based Self Theatrical Movement and later studied at the Jamaica School of Drama. He also worked for a number of years for the Sistren Theatre Collective, designing sets and costumes for them.

Mbala is a musician and a visual artist and sees himself as an artist who doesn't "separate the arts" (see interview). He also works as a percussionist with various musical ensembles like Akwaaba and the Papiumba Brass Band (with Hugh "Papi" Page).

His poetry has appeared in various anthologies like *Wheel and Come Again* and the *Oxford Book of Caribbean Poetry*, and in 2005 he published a chapbook entitled *Light in a Book of Stone.*

His poetry is both introspective and steeped in the oral tradition and can be seen as a creative synthesis of these two aspects of his art. The Caribbean oral tradition and Jamaican patois rub shoulders with an introspective streak and a concern with his "innerverse"(see interview). Art, the creative urge and the artist as wordsmith are also recurrent themes in his poetry. A certain modernist terseness characterises his poetry and brings to mind the work of William Carlos Williams.

Interview (18 August 2008, Stony Hill, Jamaica)

Interviewer: In *The Oxford Book of Caribbean Verse,* Stewart Brown and Mark McWatt defined you as a "dub and performance poet". Your poetry has appeared in different anthologies over the years, and you've been performing and writing poems for more than thirty years now. So when did you first become active as a poet

Mbala: Well when I first started to go to drama school, from those times I started scribbling down some things, you know, I started writing some stuff. That was around 1974.

I: Growing up as a kid in Jamaica, were you exposed to any type of poetry?

M: I don't have memories of doing poetry in school, you know. In high school I guess we did literature, but it was more kind of English literature, Shakespeare, stuff like that, and then I was kind of streamed as I was doing more science, maths and physics.

I: What led you to write poems eventually?

M: I was influenced more by music, or by poets that people call musicians, like Bob Dylan. Dylan was a big influence, in terms of words in the music, people like Joni Mitchell.

I: Joni Mitchell, the Canadian folk singer...

M: Yes, but Joni Mitchell grew from folk to other stuff; she just kinda morphed into a creature by herself, you know!

I: I've read somewhere that you work with musicians like Aakwaba De Drummers and the Papiumba Big Band. Tell me about these people.

M: You don't have many drummers in Jamaica. Aakwaba is a kinda loose combination of people. In fact I haven't played with them for a little while, because sometimes it's one set of people, sometimes another set, sometimes four of us, sometimes ten, it's a very flexible kind of vibes, but those guys are like *drummers!* When I play with Aakwaba I'm playing the flute, percussion, metal stuff, but those guys are *drummers*!

I: What does "aakwaba" mean?

M: It means "welcome" in some African language.

I: What about "Papiumba"?

M: Papiumba is a combination of the names of the two people in the band: I'm Mbala and the other guy is Hugh

Page and we call him "Papi". Aakwaba is a drumming group and Papiumba is more jazz-oriented, with meself on percussion and Papi on flute and sax. We also work as a total instrumental band and mostly when we work as a instrumental band, we're like ninety-eight percent improvised music, with a set-up.

I: When you perform your poetry, do you prefer working with music or just a cappella?

M: Most of the time I perform with music. I like mixing it all up. I don't like to separate arts. And I do visual arts as well, you know. I used to do silk screens and poem posters. I use visual elements with poetry.

I: I've heard that you had worked with the Jamaican company called "Sistren".

M: Yes, I used to be Sistren's set designer and I did a little costume design for them as well. I did graphics and logos.

I: How do you reach your audience? I know that you've released one CD, *Mbala* (Ricketts Production), and one chapbook, *Light in a Book of Stone* (Calabash International Literary Festival Trust, 2005).

M: I guess it's easier to reach people performance-wise, but also there are some poems which work better if you read them off the page, you know. So it depends on what the material is. There are some things that you need to kinda look at it, reread it. You just need to *see* it. Some material works better in performance, some material works on the page. But the thing is, if it's good poetry, it should work on the page if it works in performance. I find that there is some stuff out there that, when it's performed, it connects, but when you see it on the page, you can see some of the shortcomings.

I: You're primarily known as a dub or a performance poet. Are you comfortable with this "label"?

M: I really don't care one way or the other. I don't consider myself as a "dub poet" in the kind of way some people think of dub poetry, because there's a particular style that people recognise as dub poetry. It's built around a reggae rhythm, a Rasta rhythm, and it have a certain cadence to the words, a certain pattern and rhyming and stuff, right. I haven't done stuff in that kind of mainstream dub poetry vibe for a very long time.

I: So maybe the phrase"performance poet" would work better for you.

M: Yes, but at the same time, there's stuff I've done which I've put on paper. There are some poems I've written that I know I'll perform because I know they work in performance. Sometimes I just read them.

I: In the "History of Dub Poetry", you wrote about the dub poet "amusing, bemusing, confusing the centre".

M: Well, one of the roles of the dub poets, in Jamaica particulaly, is that they were like a kinda voice of the conscience. The poet to me is just like a stereo, it kinda gets inside in ways that some other forms can't reach. Poetry can seep through some little spaces and get inside your soul, you know what I mean? And the poet is there to connect with that.

I: In the same poem, you wrote about the dub poet being a "flapping dadaist, a griot, a rocking minstrel, a rapsoman and a calypso man".

M: Yes, because people sometimes get the picture that poetry cum music is something that started in Jamaica. From the dadaists to the rapsoman in Trinidad.

I: The poem entitled "History of dub poetry: take 2" lumps together "griots", "bards", "minstrels", deejays and dub poets. Are they all part of the same tradition?

M: I think so. We didn't create anything new with dub poetry.

I: As you know, in Trinidad, rapso grew out of the calypso tradition. Do you see a connection with dub poetry?

M: Yeah man, I see a connection with all that stuff, and with Brother Resistance. I saw him in one of the early videos, back in the day. He's the one who was pushing rapso.

I: In another of your poems, entitled "New Dub", you wrote that it was time to take poetry apart, and put it back together again. So was it a plea for a complete reorganisation of dub poetry?

M: It wasn't just dub poetry. It was in a sense music in general, and even life when we get stuck into some grooves more time, and we do things, and we look for formulas, so this a hit, and every hit starts to sound like that, which is why I find popular music so boring. And these people sell millions and millions of records; that's kinda boring, because they use the same formula. You know, I can listen to one piece of music, I've never heard it before, and I'm whispering along with it. I'm humming along because I know where it's going. Same pattern, same formula. Boring!

I: In a way, the same thing happened to dub poetry. It fell into a kind of routine, and everyone started doing the same thing.

M: Yeah, and not only that, because the pattern is one thing, but people have taken the pattern and done things with it, but some people tend to just regurgitate stuff that Okunonuora, Linton [Kwesi Johnson] have said before many times, and said better.

You have some clichés that keep coming out: everything is in "-tion", "it's time for libera*tion*", "me naw want no frustra*tion*", du du du du du. That's doing a disservice to poetry, I think. It's the same for other art forms. There's always been people who have been doing stuff with the form that's really creative and others who just imitate. Sometimes, the crafting of the poetry gets short-changed.

I: What about the status of dub or performance poetry today in Jamaica? Do you think there's an audience for it, a new generation, or is it something which is more associated with the 1980s or the 1970s?

M: It's still associated with the 1970s, but it's still around. I mean, what you'll find is that Like the JCDC [Jamaica Cultural Development Committee) has a kind of festival thing in the performing arts category and you have school kids doing dub poetry. They do a good job with the performance aspect, and the kids perform very, very well, but a lot of the time, the words, the patterns, the subject matter tend to be the same stuff: fighting against oppression, our people are suffering. There's a sameness to it, even if it's *well done*.

I: What about the main venues for poetry in Jamaica? Are there many venues available to poets?

M: I don't know if you'll find that much mainstream performance of poetry. You'll probably find Cherry Natural on some shows with reggae artists and stuff. There's smaller venues like the Poetry Society of Jamaica; we meet every last Tuesday at the School of Drama, and we've been doing that from 1989. We facilitate a fellowship, sometimes we have a featured poet.

I: I've noticed that you use a kind of semi-phonetic spelling sometimes, but your poems are not in patois.

M: Well, in terms of writing the language, there's a system called the Le Page and Cassidy phonemic system , but I'm not familiar with that. I kinda use a bastardised system, because some English words are the same as the patois words.

I: Do you write in Standard English?

M: I do write in Standard English. "Mundane" is in Standard English. Quite a few are in Standard English, but I write in patois as well, because Jamaicans tend to switch depending on who you're talking to. When I'm talking to you, I talk like this, and when I talk to somebody else, I use a more raw kinda patois. You don't really think about it, you tailor your speech to who you're talking to, and therefore there's a whole spectrum of what you call ways of speaking. But I like to use patois because I think that people tend to think sometimes that there are things that can't express in patois. Some people use patois in dub poetry to talk about the suffering, but I feel you can use patois to talk about anything. You can get abstract.

I: How do you make a decision to write in Jamaican patois or in Standard English? Is it to do with the subject matter of the poem, the way you feel at a particular moment?

M: I'm not sure how this really works.Subject matter is a factor but sometimes a poem will start out on one side of the language line and end up on the other side, and some even include both English and patois in the same poem. And jamaican patois can be quite close to English.

Perhaps in terms of subject matter, patois can deal with certain things, especially certain Jamaican t'ings, in ways that English just cannot handle. There are shades of meanings, nuances that because of cultural or historical codes in the language just don't have exact English translations.

I think this is true for all languages. With traditional dub poetry patois has tended to deal with a more limited range of subjects like protest, revolution, social commentry, but I have always thought that it could be used to express even the most profound thoughts and feelings, and I've always tried to do this (for instance in "snake of paradise", which mixes in a little English, "wud boom" and "pbb") but words are words and I just love romping with them, English, patois or Martian!

I: "Mundane" was inspired by several paintings by René Magritte, and the first section of the poem, entitled "mundane", was inspired by "Les valeurs personnelles". Do you see this painting as some kind of personal manifesto that applies to poetry too? How did you first become interested in

Surrealism?

M: Art is important to me as a poet, as a visual artist, musician, as a human being. I love Surrealism perhaps because as in poetry there is so much beneath the surface, and Magritte, with his quite conservative method of painting, has such a quiet still other-worldly feel.

Maybe this is what I want my poems to be like: ordinary words with a whole other universe under their skins.

I'm interested in the differences between the outer or public space and our inner or personal spaces, the exploration of the "life within a life". This painting does it for me, and I think this is what I want poetry to do: to look at the mundane and see the fantastic underneath.

I grew up reading a lot, but especially comics and science fiction where imagination was allowed to run free to go deep, deep beneath skin and light years beyond skin (like poetry!). I guess that's why I like Surrealism and things on the edge where the "truth that dodges reason" lives.

I: "shallows" seems to describe the artist's task: to go under the surface of things and come up with something new. Is every poem a challenge? The last word, "seachange", is an echo from *The Tempest* by Shakespeare.

M: I've had a thing with that word since I worked on a production of *The Tempest* and I did a piece of artwork (a mask) called "seachange". I think it's the task of every human being, not just artists, to live under the surface, to be aware and connected to our own personal innerverse, even if we don't come up with something 'new', though for the artist it is a challenge to not repeat the same things too often.

I: The poem entitled "dj lovesong" is obviously critical of some dancehall artists' attitude towards women. It cleverly recycles the titles of some famous dancehall tunes. When did you write this piece?

M: I think that was 2008. I am concerned with the treatment of women (I used to be labelled the "feminist environmentalist poet") and I work with a group called Women's Media Watch trying to sensitise (especially young) people about gender issues.

I use the poem in some of our workshops and as a musician (as a human being). I just can't understand how people (including the deejays themselves) don't see the ridiculous and dangerous contradiction going on here.

I: "autobio" seems to warn against too much autobiography in poetry. Should the poet avoid autobiographical elements?

M: I don't think the poet should avoid autobiography. After all, the human story is universal. What the artist has lived is what the reader has lived, though personally I really don't need that much detail, and I don't think people need too much of the details of my life either. With "autobio" I was also just having a bit of fun (while trying to remain truthful).

CONCLUSION

Several important themes run through these interviews and may help us to understand the view from the grassroots. First, the poets interviewed all acknowledge a tremendous debt of gratitude to Louise Bennett, aka, Miss Lou, the godmother of dub poetry so to speak. Miss Lou's wit and poems in Creole seem to have inspired these poets to take up the pen or to raise their voices. In an interview granted to Susan Gingell, the Jamaican-Canadian poet ahdri zhina mandiela said that Miss Lou's TV programme *Dr Ring Ding* had been a major source of inspiration for her, as had been the work done by Ranny Williams, Miss Lou's collaborator on stage (Gingell 2006). Yasus Afari and Malachi D Smith both consider Miss Lou as their poetic "mother". Mutabaruka actually worked with Louise Bennett and took her to a recording studio where "she ride the riddim wicked!" (see interview) to lay tracks for the *Woman Talk* LP. Kokumo fondly remembers watching *Dr Ring Ding* on TV every Saturday and remembers reciting some Louise Bennett poems at school.

Secondly, the role played by teachers in the nurturing of young talent in the crucial decades that followed independence in Jamaica cannot be overemphasised. By encouraging their pupils to perform their own poems or Louise Bennet's poems or by urging them to write, they contributed enormously to the growth of poetic talent in Jamaica. Malachi D. Smith and Cherry Natural were both encouraged to read Claude Mc Kay's poems at school. McKay was one of the first Caribbean poets to use the vernacular in his poetry and his two poetry collections, *Constab Ballads* (1912) and *Songs of Jamaica* (1912) seem to have been very influential with budding poets.

Thirdly, some of these poets seem to agree on the "activist frame" (Bucknor 2011) in which dub poetry is to be situated. Dub poetry is to be the "voice of the downtrodden" according to Kokumo Noxid and Cherry Natural defines herself as an "activist". Mutabruka insists on the need to change mentalities which he sees dominated by politics and religion. Most of these poets see dub poetry as a revolutionary tool for change.

Another imporant theme which emerges from these interviews is the use of dub poetry as a pedagogical instrument, as a teaching aid, as underlined by Klyde Broox and Dreadlockalien. Dub poetry is thus considered as a powerful force in education too. Cherry Natural has conducted workshops with "sex workers" and pregnant women. Dreadlockalien and Klyde Broox have worked in schools and conducted workshops there at certain periods of their lives.

So where is dub poetry going in 2017?

As Klyde Broox told me after I interviewed him in Canada, as long as there is one dub poet alive and performing, then dub poetry is alive. Judged from this perspective, dub poetry is alive and well. Indeed, Malachi D Smith has just released a new CD in Miami (*Wiseman*), Kokumo Noxid's collection of poems, *Dub Truth*, was published in England in 2016, and Cherry Natural relcased a new CD, *Intellectual Bad Gal*, a few years ago.

Yasus Afari organises a poetry spot in Mandeville once a month, the Poetry Society of Jamaica holds a fellowship every last Tuesday of every month at the Edna Manley College of the Visual and Performing Arts, and Klyde Broox regularly organises poetry readings in his adopted hometown Hamilton, Ontario. Mutabaruka perfoms regularly and his radio show, *The Cutting Edge*, has proved extremely popular in Jamaica and all over the world (see interview). In 2014, Oku Onuora released a new CD, *A Movement*, with Sly and Robbie and Monty Alexander.

So many dub poets are active and performing regularly, but some of them like Kokumo and Malachi Smith point out that the media tend to ignore dub poetry and that even though the art form is popular at the "grassroots level" as Malachi Smith said, it lacks official recognition and support from the media. Moqapi Selassie tends to think that dub poetry has been let down by some of its own practitioners and that the art form is struggling to survive. Mbala seems or seemed to think that dub poetry has become too repetitive, relying on a set of clichés and formulas instead of introducing new strategies.

Over the years, attempts have been made to federate dub poets and encourage them to work together (for instance, Poets in Unity in the 1970s in Jamaica; the Conscious Poets Society and the New October Poets in England in the 1990s; the Dub Poets Collective in Toronto), but these have tended to work for short periods only.

Nevertheless, dub poetry continues to survive in diasporic communities all over the world and in Jamaica. In Jamaica, a new generation seems to have appeared with Jawara Ellis, Ras Takura, Sage, Charlie Bobus among others and Toronto has the largest concentration of dub poets outside Jamaica with Lillian Allen, Klyde Broox, Michael St George, d'b young, ahdri zinia mandiela and Afua Cooper among others. Oku Onuora, the founding father of the movement, takes the optimisitc view that the spoken word and performance poetry scene is vibrant in Jamaica today.

Finally it must be recognised that dub poetry has also changed over the years and slowly morphed into spoken word or slam with new poets like Kokumo Noxid, Dreadlocklien and Yasus Afari. It hasn't ceased to exist but simply taken new forms.

BIBLIOGRAPHY

Afari, Yasus.

Eye Pen. Kingston: House of Honour Publishing, 1998.

Overstanding Rastafari: Jamaica's Gift to the World, 2007.

Vocal Ink: The Mental Intercourse. Kingston: Senya-Cum, 2016. ---------------.

Allen, Lillian.

Rhythm An' Hardtimes. Toronto: Verse to Vinyl, 1982.

Women Do This Every Day. Toronto: Women's Press, 1993.

Psychic Unrest. Toronto: Insomniac Press, 1999.

Batson-Savage, Tanya.

"Intellectual Bad Gyal Unleashed at Poetry Society". *Susumba*. July 1st 2013.

Brathwaite, Edward Kamau.

The History of the Voice:The Development of Nation Language in Anglophone Caribbean Poetry. Londres : New Beacon Books,1984.

Breeze, Jean Binta.

Riddim Ravings. London: Race Today, 1988.

Third World Girl: Selected Poems. Highgreen: Bloodaxe Books, 2011.

Broox, Klyde.

Poemstorm. Kingston, 1989.

My Best Friend is White. Toronto: Klyde Broox, 2005.

Brown, Stewart.

"Dub Poetry: Selling Out", *Poetry Wales*,vol. 22.2, 1987.

Brown, Stewart, Mervyn Morris and Gordon Rohlher.

Voiceprint: An Anthology of Oral and Related Poetry from the Caribbean. Harlow: Longman, 1989.

Brown, Stewart et Mark McWatt, eds.

The Oxford Book of Caribbean Verse. Oxford: Oxford University Press, 2005.

Bucknor, Michael A. and Alison Donnell, eds.

The Routledge Companion to Anglophone Caribbean Literature. London: Routledge, 2011.

Bucknor, Michael A.

"Dub Poetry as a Postmodern Art Form Self-Concious of Critical Recxeption", in Michael A. Bucknor and Alison Donnell, eds, *The Routledge Companion to Anglophone Caribbean Literature*. London: Routledge, 2011.

Burnett, Paula, ed.
The Penguin Book of Caribbean Verse in English. London: Penguin, 1986.

Casas, Maria Caridad,
"Whose Rhythm? Textualized Riddim in Lillian Allen's *Women Do This Every Day*", *Essays on Canadian Writing*, 2004.

Chang, Victor.
Review of Christian Habekost (ed.), *Dub Poetry: 19 Poets from England and Jamaica*, in *Jamaica Journal*, 21.3, 1986.

Cooke, Mel.
"Oku Onuora launches 'A Movement'". *The Gleaner*. 3 June 2013.

Cooper, Carolyn
Noises in the Blood: Orality, Gender and the Vulgar Body of Jamaican Popular Culture. London: Macmillan Caribbean, 1993.

Dawes, Kwame, ed.
Wheel and Come Again: An Anthtology of Reggae Poetry. Leeds: Peepal Tree Press, 1998.

Doumerc, Eric and Roy MacFarlane, eds.
Celebrate Wha: Ten Black British Poets from the Midlands. Middlesbrough: Smokestacks Books, 2011.

Gingell, Susan.
"Always a Poem, Once a Book": Motivations and Strategies for Print Textualizing of Caribbean-Canadian Dub and Performance Poetry", *The Journal of West Indian Literature*, Vol 14 (1 and 2), 2005.
"jumping in heart first - an interview with ahdri zhina mandiela". *Postcolonial Text*, Vol 2, N° 4 (2006).

Glaser, Marlies and Marion Pausch, eds.
Caribbean Writers: Between Orality and Writing. Amsterdam and Atlanta: Rodopi, 1994.

Habekost,Christian.

Dub Poetry: 19 Poets from England and Jamaica. Neuestadt: Michael Schwinn, 1986.

*Verbal Riddim: The Politics and Aesthetics of African-Jamaican Dub Poetry.*Amsterdam and Atlanta: Rodopi, 1993.

Johnson, Linton Kwesi.

Voices of the Living and the Dead. London: Race Today, 1974.

Dread Beat an' Blood. London: Bogle L'Ouverture, 1975.

"Jamaican Rebel Music". *Race and Class*, vol.17, n°4, 1976.

Inglan is a Bitch. London; Race Today Publication, 1980, reprinted 1981, 1987.

Selected Poems. London: Penguin Books, 2002.

"Writing Reggae: Poetry, Politics and Popular Culture", *Jamaica Journal* Vol.33, Nos 1-2 (December 2010).

Markham, E.A. *Hinterland*

Caribbean Poetry from the West Indies and Britain. Newcastle: Bloodaxe Books, 1989.

Miller, Kei.

A Smaller Sound, a Lesser Fury: a Eulogy for Dub Poetry, m2.facebook.com

Mordecai, Pamela.

"The Labels Pin them down – An Interview with Mervyn Morris", in *Caribbean Writers – Between Orality and Writing*, eds Marlies Glaser and Marion Pausch Amsterdam and Atlanta: Rodopi, 1994.

Morley, Jonathan

"Dub Poetry", in Dabydeen, David, J.Gilmore and C. Jones, eds, *The Oxford Companion to Black British History.* Oxford: Oxford University Press, 2007.

Morris, Mervyn

"People's Speech", in Stephen Davis and Peter Simon, *Reggae International.* London: Thames and Hudson, 1983.

"The Poetry of Mikey Smith.", in *West Indian Literature and its Social Context*, edited by Mark McWatt, Cave Hill, Barbados: University of the West Indies, 1988.

"Interview with Michael Smith.", in *Hinterland: Caribbean*

Poetry from the West Indies and Britain, Newcastle Upon Tyne: Bloodaxe Books, 1989.
"A Note on Dub Poetry". *Wasafiri*, 25, 1997.

Mutabaruka
Mutabaruka: The First Poems, Neustadt: Michael Schwinn,1987.
The First Poems/ The Next Poems. Kingston: Paul Issa Publications, 2005.

Natural, Cherry.
Come Meck We Reason. Kingston: Careso/Volunteers Social Service, 1989.
Earth Woman – Selected Poems 1989-2001.Bloomington, Indiana: Rastazumska Productions, 2003.

Noxid, Kokumo.
Dub Truth. APS Publications, 2016

Onuora, Oku
Echo. Kingston: Sangster's, 1977.

Smith, Michael.
It A Come. London: Race Today, 1986.

Walters, Basil.
"Yasus Afari Launches New Book", *The Jamaica Obsever*. 9 April 2016.

Zephaniah, Benjamin.
Pen Rhythm. London: Page One, 1980.
The Dread Affair. London: Akira Press, 1985.
City Psalms. Newcastle upon Tyne: Bloodaxe Books, 1992.
Propa Propaganda.Newcastle upon Tyne:Bloodaxe Books, 1996.
Too Black, Too Strong. Newcastle upon Tyne: Bloodaxe Books, 2001.

DISCOGRAPHY

Various Artists:

Dread Poets Society: The Anthology of Contemporary Dub Poetry, CD, T'Bwana Sounds, 1993.

Woman Talk: Caribbean Dub Poetry, LP, Heartbeat, 1986.

Word Sound 'Ave Power: Reggae Poetry, LP, Heartbeat, 1983.

Afari, Yasus.

Dancehall Baptism, CD, Tappa Zukie, 1993.

Mental Assassin, CD, Senya-Cum, 1995.

Honour Crown Him, CD, Senya-Cum, 1997.

Jamaica's Gift of Vision, CD, Senya-Cum, 2000.

Revolution Chapter 1, CD, Senya-Cum, 2007.

Public Secret, CD, Senya-Cum, 2013.

Allen, Lillian

Revolutionary Tea Party, LP, Verse to Vinyl, 1986.

Conditions Critical, LP, Verse to Vinyl, 1988.

Anxiety, CD, Verse to Vinyl, 2012.

Breeze, Jean Binta,

Tracks, LP , LKJ, 1988.

Johnson, Linton Kwesi.

Dread Beat and Blood, LP, Virgin, 1978.

Forces of Victory, cassette, Island, 1979.

Bass Culture, LP, Island, 1980.

Making History, LP, Island 1984.

In Concert with the Dub Band, cassette, Shanachie, 1985.

Tings An' Times, cassette, FNAC, 1991.

More Time, CD, LKJ Records, 1998.

Kokumo

Writing's on the Wall, CD, Abeng Prod, 2006.

Mbala

Mbala, CD, Ricketts Productions.

Mutabaruka

Check it! cassette, Ada, 1983.

Outcry cassette, Shanachie, 1984.

The Mystery Unfolds, Shanachie, LP, 1986.

Any which way...Freedom, Shanachie, cassette, 1989.

Blakk Wi Black...k...k, Shanachie, cassette, 1991.
Natural, Cherry
Memoirs of a Praying Mantis, CD, Bamboo Media.
Earth Woman, CD, Virquarian Music, 1999.
Intellectual Bad Gal, CD, 2013.
Onuora, Oku
Pressure Drop, LP, Blue Moon, 1985.
I A Tell Dubwize and Otherwise, cassette, ROIR, 1991.
Buss Out, LP, Blue Moon, 1993.
A Movement, 2013 (I Tunes).
Ras Mo
Tjébé/Hold On, CD, Mo'N'Mo Music, 1998.
Smith, Malachi D.
Throw Two Punch, 1998.
The Blacker the Berry, The Sweeter the Cherry, 2001
Middle Passage, CD, 4-M Music, 2003.
Luv Dub Fever, CD, 4-M Music, 2008.
Hail to Jamaica, CD, 4-M Records, 2010.
Scream, CD, 4-M Music, 2014.
Wiseman, CD, Upstairs Music, 2017.
Smith, Michael
Mi Cyaan Believe It, LP, Island, 1982.
Zephaniah, Benjamin
Dub Ranting, 45 rpm, Radical Wallpaper, 1982.
Rasta, LP, Upright, 1983.
Free South Africa,,LP, Upright, 1986.
Us and Dem, cassette, Mango/Island, 1990.
Overstanding, cassette, Benjamin Zephaniah Associates, 1992.
Back to Roots, CD, Acid Jazz Records, 1995.
Belly of the Beast, CD, Ariwa, 1996.

Eric Doumerc teaches English at the University of Toulouse-Jean Jaurès, southwestern France. His research interests include Caribbean poetry, music, and the Caribbean oral tradition. He edited *Five Birmingham Poets,* an anthology of poems by black poets from the West Midlands which was published in 2006 by Raka Books, the late Roi Kwabena's publishing imprint. In 2011, Smokestack Books published *Celebrate Wha': Ten Black British Poets from the Midlands* (Middelesbrough: Smokestack Books, 2011), an anthology which he co-edited with the poet Roy McFarlane. He is also the author of 'Jamaican Music In England' published by APS Books in 2018.

www.ingramcontent.com/pod-product-compliance
Ingram Content Group UK Ltd.
Pitfield, Milton Keynes, MK11 3LW, UK
UKHW021918190726
13853UKWH00002B/734